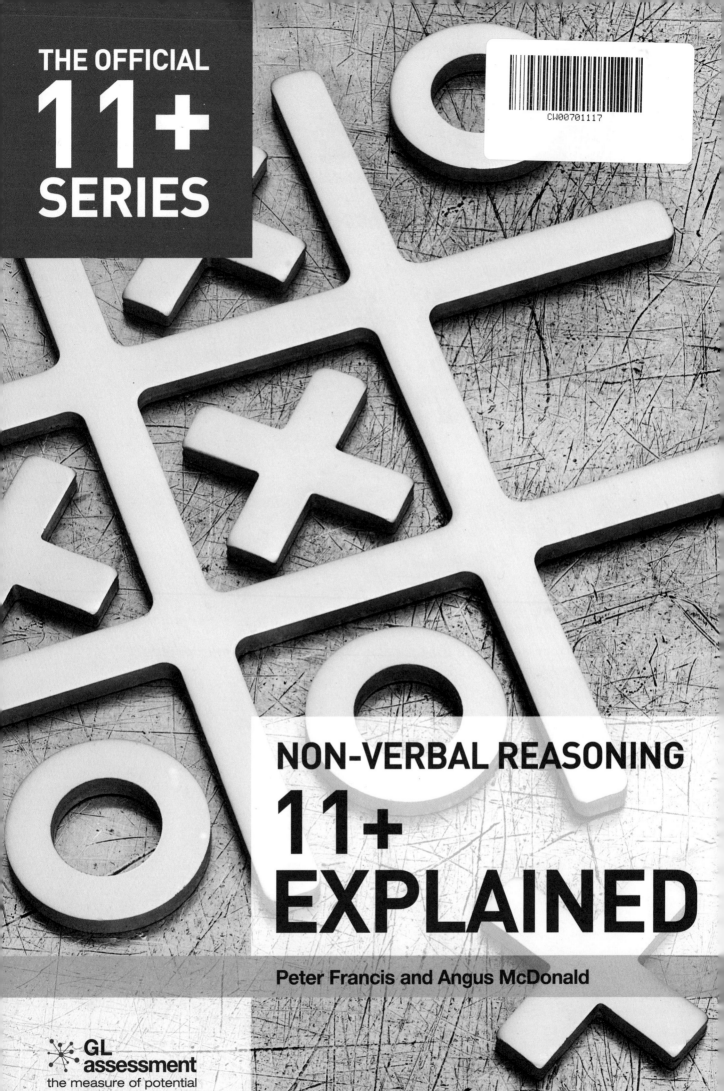

THE OFFICIAL 11+ SERIES

CW00701117

NON-VERBAL REASONING
11+
EXPLAINED

Peter Francis and Angus McDonald

GL assessment
the measure of potential

THE OFFICIAL 11+ PRACTICE SERIES

11+ Explained

The Official Parents' Guide to the 11+

11+ Practice Papers

The Official 11+ website: www.officialelevenplus.co.uk

Offering further information and advice for parents, and digital practice tests

Copyright © 2011 GL Assessment Limited

Published by GL Assessment Limited

389 Chiswick High Road, 9th Floor East, London, W4 4AL

www.gl-assessment.co.uk

GL Assessment is part of the Granada Learning Group

Designed and typeset by Starfish Design, Editorial and Project Management Ltd
Cover photo: David Muir/Digital Vision/Getty Images

ISBN 978 0 7087 2054 7

1(4.11)

CONTENTS

HOW TO USE THIS BOOK

- **WHAT ARE THE AIMS OF THIS BOOK?**
- **WHAT'S IN THE BOOK?**
- **WHAT WILL I LEARN?**
- **HOW DO I USE THIS BOOK?**

WHAT ARE THE AIMS OF THIS BOOK?

Welcome to the *11+ Explained*! This book will help you develop the skills you need to do your best in the 11+ Non-Verbal Reasoning test. It makes your 11+ learning interesting and fun.

Improve your test technique

Learn how to do each question type

11+ success

Strengthen your skills with games and activities

Practise 11+ style questions

Check your progress to build your confidence

WHAT'S IN THE BOOK?

Part 1: Getting ready for the 11+
These short chapters tell you about the 11+ and help you improve your skills. First, we explain about the 11+ test. Then we show you how to check your progress and develop your test technique. There are also some tips to use in your final preparation, to make sure you do your best in the actual 11+ test.

Part 2: Non-Verbal Reasoning question types explained
This step-by-step guide to the 11+ Non-Verbal Reasoning question types will help you answer each question type successfully. It gives you tips on answering the questions and fun activities to practise the skills you need. There are also some tips for your parents or carers, so that they can help you even more.

WHAT ARE PARENT TIPS?

Parent Tips suggest how your parent or carer could help you. Sometimes they provide further information on the question type. Sometimes they show activities to help you develop skills to solve the question quickly and accurately. Only read them if you want to!

WHAT WILL I LEARN?

The *11+ Explained* shows you the 8 question types that can appear in the 11+ Non-Verbal Reasoning tests. All 11+ Non-Verbal Reasoning tests will use some of these question types, but they won't always use all of them. You will learn how to approach each question type and also develop your confidence and skills.

HOW DO I USE THIS BOOK?

Why not read through Part 1 of this book with your parent or carer so that you can find out about the 11+ together?

You can use this book in the best way for you. This chart shows you one good way to go through the book to make sure you do things in a helpful order. Each chapter and each question type in this book can also be read on its own.

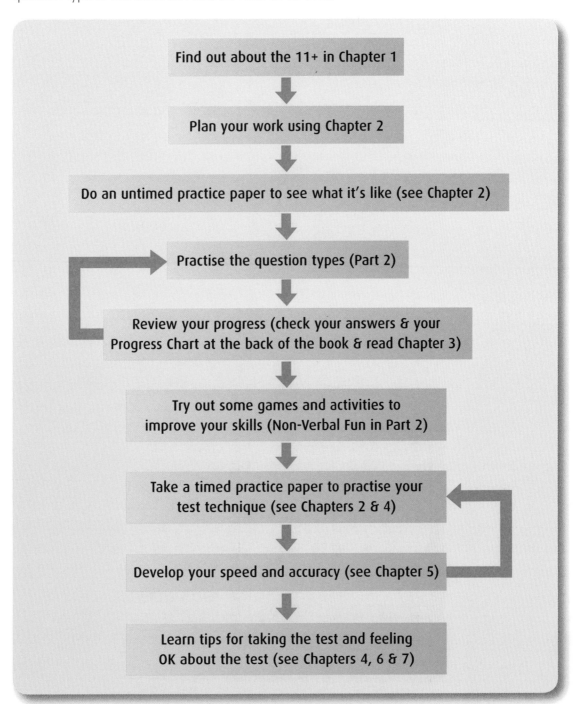

Find out about the 11+ in Chapter 1

Plan your work using Chapter 2

Do an untimed practice paper to see what it's like (see Chapter 2)

Practise the question types (Part 2)

Review your progress (check your answers & your Progress Chart at the back of the book & read Chapter 3)

Try out some games and activities to improve your skills (Non-Verbal Fun in Part 2)

Take a timed practice paper to practise your test technique (see Chapters 2 & 4)

Develop your speed and accuracy (see Chapter 5)

Learn tips for taking the test and feeling OK about the test (see Chapters 4, 6 & 7)

Working through a question type

Question types using similar skills are grouped together in a coloured section

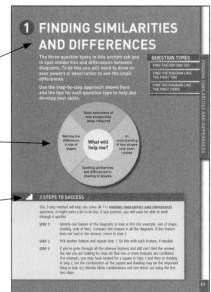

Skills you will need to develop

Each question type shows you 3 steps to help you work out the answers

Key words used

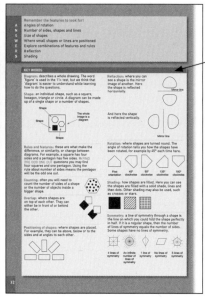

Tells you about the question type and what skills you need

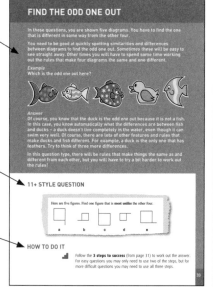

Try an 11+ style question

Work through the step-by-step instructions, using the **3 steps to success** for each section

Tips can help you avoid making common mistakes and can save you time

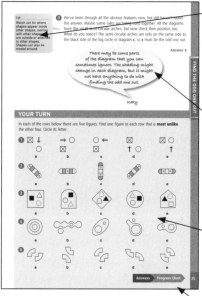

Quotes from other children who have taken the 11+ provide useful advice on the question type you've just learned

Try practice questions to make sure you know what to do

Check your answers and record your score on the Progress Chart at the back of the book – check how well you are doing and what you need to practise more

Try the activities and games to build your skills – do some of these with a friend or family member

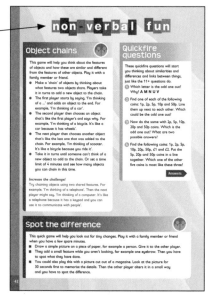

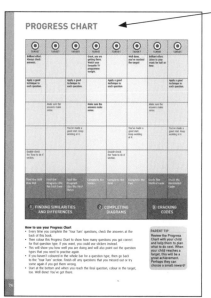

Find out more about the *11+ test* on page 6

4

PART 1

Getting ready for the 11+

- **WHAT ARE 11+ TESTS USED FOR?**
- **WHAT IS NON-VERBAL REASONING?**

WHAT ARE 11+ TESTS USED FOR?

The 11+ test is used by some secondary schools to help decide which pupils to select.
11+ tests can include some or all of the following tests:

- English
- Maths
- Non-Verbal Reasoning
- Verbal Reasoning

This book is about the Non-Verbal Reasoning tests that many schools use.

PARENT TIP   How can I help my child?

To find out which tests are used in your area, look at our 11+ website:
www.officialelevenplus.co.uk.

THE NAME OF THE TEST

The tests you're preparing for are often called '11+' or 'Eleven Plus' tests. This name was used when the tests were first introduced, more than 60 years ago. Some schools now use modern names such as 'selection' or 'admissions' tests.

In this book, we use the name '11+' or '11+ test'.

WHAT IS NON-VERBAL REASONING?

Non-Verbal Reasoning is about the ability to solve problems using pictures and shapes.

Non-Verbal Reasoning is included in many 11+ tests as it shows how well you can solve problems and learn new ideas.

Developing your Non-Verbal Reasoning skills will also help you at school by:
- helping you to become a better learner
- encouraging you to come up with ideas and solve problems
- making you more confident when faced with new information and ideas.

This sort of question may be new to you, unless you have already done some Non-Verbal Reasoning tests at school. So here we are going to show you what it's all about!

Non-Verbal Reasoning explained

Non-Verbal Reasoning is all about using your detective skills to solve problems using patterns and shapes.

You already do this, even if you don't know it! For example, when you see your friends you know who they are straight away. Something about their face or clothes makes them different from any other friend. On the other hand, sometimes we don't notice even if they have had their hair cut!

When you walk into a room at home, do you notice when something has been moved around? Sometimes you just know that the room seems different from how it was when you went to school that morning and now you are trying to spot what has changed.

Understanding Non-Verbal Reasoning is a bit like this – you have to start noticing changes that you might not have bothered looking at before. When you are doing Non-Verbal Reasoning questions, you will have to think about things like shapes, shading and numbers.

You will notice straight away that Non-Verbal Reasoning questions look different from most other questions you will have come across before. You will see that different shapes and patterns are used to make diagrams quite unlike any you see in other tests or at school.

This means that the way you will work out the answers to these types of questions will be a bit different too. This book will show you how.

Get ready!

Let's look at some of the shapes and patterns all around us to help get ready to tackle Non-Verbal Reasoning questions.

Look around you. How many different shapes can you see? You might see a square window and a circular table. Are there any triangles in the room? Try to spot different shapes in the furniture or the wallpaper or carpets.

Can you see a door? Look at where the door handle is – is it on the right of the door? Go round the door and look at it from the other side. Do you see that the door handle is now on the left? When this happens in a drawing, like the one below, it is called *reflection*. Try to remember this sort of thinking when you do Non-Verbal Reasoning questions, as many will use reflection in the diagrams.

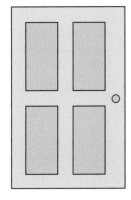 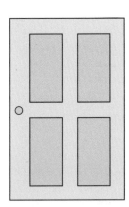

Now take a look at the different patterns that we see in everyday things all around us. Look at some tins of food. Each tin will probably have a different number of circles of different sizes on the bottom. Count them. Do any have the same number of circles on the bottom? When you do an 'odd one out' type of question you will have to look for things that are the same or different.

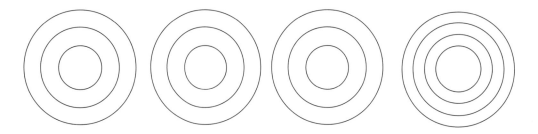

Now think about a clock and imagine the hands showing 1 o'clock, 3 o'clock, 5 o'clock and 7 o'clock. What pattern do the short hand and long hand make at each of these times? What changes between 1 o'clock and 3 o'clock, between 3 o'clock and 5 o'clock, and between 5 o'clock and 7 o'clock? We know there is two hours' difference between each of these times, but how do the hands change between these times?

If we draw just the hands of the clock without the clock face, it would look something like this:

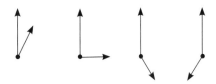

This pattern of clock hands is like some of the Non-Verbal Reasoning questions you will learn to solve in this book. However, you won't be told that they are clock hands or that there is meant to be two hours' difference between each. The challenge will be to look at diagrams such as these and work out the relationship between them by thinking about things such as angles and rotation. When you know how the different diagrams are linked, you will then have to use this information to solve problems like choosing which diagram comes next.

Some of the Non-Verbal Reasoning questions you will come across include things like shapes, pattern, reflection, counting, angles and rotation. If you start looking out for these things in the world around you, it will help you with the questions.

PARENT TIP   How can I help my child?

The *11+ Explained* is designed for children to be able to use without a lot of parental guidance but, as a parent, you play a vital role in supporting your child as they prepare for the 11+ test.

Many of the activities suggested in this book need two people and these provide a perfect opportunity to guide and support your child through the book and the 11+ process. Sharing this experience can enable both parents and child to feel a sense of achievement.

It's particularly important for you to:
- help your child develop a realistic preparation plan and revise it, if necessary
- encourage your child to review their plan regularly, check their progress and recognise their successes
- motivate your child by giving praise and encouragement, and by providing appropriate rewards
- provide ongoing support and specific advice when needed, such as checking answers and working on their test technique
- help your child understand and manage the emotions that accompany a challenge such as the 11+ test
- work to build and maintain your child's confidence throughout the preparation process, as confidence is essential for good performance
- make sure that your child takes regular breaks and gets plenty of fresh air and exercise, as well as eating and sleeping well.

More detailed guidance on how to support your child is provided in GL Assessment's *Official Parents' Guide to the 11+* (see front of book).

Find out how to *plan your 11+* work on the next page

2 PLANNING MY 11+ PREPARATION

- **HOW MUCH TIME WILL I NEED?**
- **HOW SHOULD I PLAN MY WORK?**
- **DO I NEED ANY OTHER RESOURCES?**
- **WHEN SHOULD I USE PRACTICE PAPERS?**

HOW MUCH TIME WILL I NEED?

Any time you spend preparing for the 11+ test will be helpful but, ideally, give yourself at least 3 months to work through the question types in the *11+ Explained*. To give yourself plenty of time, we recommend that you start preparing 6 or even 12 months before the test.

Each question type in the *11+ Explained* should take around 30 to 45 minutes. You will learn about the question type, then you can try the practice questions and do the Non-Verbal Fun activities. You will probably also want to revisit each question type later on, to check your understanding and develop your test technique.

You will have to work more quickly if you don't start preparing until nearer your test date. For example:

- if you have 12 months, try to do one Non-Verbal Reasoning question type about every 3 or 4 weeks
- if you have 6 months, you may need to try one Non-Verbal Reasoning question type about every 2 weeks.

PARENT TIP   How can I help my child organise their preparation time?

To prepare fully for the 11+, your child needs to do many things, including:
- learning about the different question types and how to solve them
- learning how to apply techniques and strategies
- practising and reviewing individual question types
- trying full 11+ practice papers under both timed and untimed conditions to develop their test technique
- learning strategies for the actual test and following the final tips for preparation.

Your child should focus on each of these activities at different points in their preparation. The 'right' amount of time spent on each activity will vary from child to child, depending on their abilities and rate of learning.

As a parent, you can help most by monitoring your child's progress on each activity carefully and encouraging them to move on to other activities when they have reached a reasonable level of skill. You may also want to move your child on to another activity if they are finding something particularly difficult, and then return to it later.

See also *The Official Parents' Guide to the 11+* (Chapter 6)

HOW SHOULD I PLAN MY WORK?

The best way to use this book is as part of a preparation plan that builds towards the 11+ test. You need to be organised to give yourself the best chance of success, so a timetable will help.

WORK WITH YOUR PARENT OR CARER

- It's better if you work together with your parent or carer to help you develop your timetable.
- Your parent or carer will be able to suggest how long to spend on each activity and will check that your timetable is realistic.
- You can also agree on the 'success points' (your goals) and rewards for reaching them.

Your timetable should give you an outline of what activities you will be doing and when. But it needs to be flexible because the time you spend on each activity will depend on:

- how much time you have
- how well you understand the different question types
- how quickly you develop your test technique.

Make sure that you include time for:

- learning how to do each question type and doing the practice questions
- doing the Non-Verbal Fun activities
- checking you understand each question type
- getting to know the tips for each question type and developing your test technique
- preparing for the actual test.

How long you spend on each of these will depend on your own needs. But here's a suggested breakdown of how you might spend your time if you have 12 months to prepare:

Checking you understand the question types and developing your test technique (about 20 weeks)

Learning how to do the question types (about 30 weeks)

Final preparation for the test day (about 2 weeks)

PARENT TIP   How can I help my child draw up a timetable?

- Start by working out how long it is to their 11+ test and work back from there.
- Make sure your child has plenty of time for learning about all the question types – we recommend roughly two-thirds of the total time is spent on this.
- Once they have covered most of the question types, they should start reviewing their progress by looking at their Progress Chart and identifying any question types that need further work.
- They should then spend time on taking practice papers, working on speed and accuracy, learning test technique and trying out the games and activities.

See also *The Official Parents' Guide to the 11+* (Chapter 9)

Using the timetable

Why not tick off the activities on your timetable when you have done them? This will let you see at a glance how much of your preparation you have completed. You should also colour in the Progress Chart at the back of the book to help you see how you are getting on.

Perhaps your parent or carer will give you a reward when you complete a question type successfully!

PARENT TIP   How should I reward my child's successes?

An important part of developing a preparation plan with your child is to identify 'success points' and what rewards your child may receive when they reach them. Rewards play an important part in recognising the effort that your child has put into their preparation so far and also motivating them to continue with their preparation.

Reward your child mainly **for their effort not their achievement** because children's potential varies. However, since effort is one of the main factors that will determine how well an individual will do on the test, if you reward effort and encourage them to try harder, then greater achievement will naturally follow.

The more children can 'reward themselves' by recognising their own achievements, the more motivated they are likely to be. Simple rewards such as praise and getting them to evaluate just how far they have come and what they have achieved by reviewing their plan and Progress Chart can be a great way to do this. Parents should regularly give this type of reward.

Giving treats will be important at times, but you can reward your child in other ways too. You will know what your child enjoys, and so this will be the best starting point for identifying appropriate rewards. Ideas include spending time on hobbies or with family and friends, watching a favourite TV programme, playing on a computer and having trips out.

See also *The Official Parents' Guide to the 11+* (Chapter 10)

DO I NEED ANY OTHER RESOURCES?

The *11+ Explained* gives you all the information you need to understand the Non-Verbal Reasoning test and how to approach it.

You will also need:
- pens and pencils (different colours will help)
- plenty of spare paper
- a clock or stopwatch (for timing yourself on practice papers and for some Non-Verbal Fun activities)
- 11+ practice papers – these are not included in this book, but are very important to help you develop your test technique.

DO NOT DISTURB!

You will need a quiet place to work in. This is especially important when practising questions and taking timed practice tests. Let your family know when you will be working and ask them not to disturb you. Try putting a sign on the door or working in your local library if it's too noisy at home.

WHEN SHOULD I USE PRACTICE PAPERS?

Practice papers are an important part of preparation. They will help you:
- understand what the 11+ test will be like
- spot the question types you find most difficult and may need to look at again
- get used to answering questions quickly and accurately, within the time limit for the test
- develop your test technique.

When to do practice papers

Practice papers are the best way to experience what your actual 11+ test will be like, so make sure you include some in your preparation plan.

Take an **untimed practice paper** early on in your preparation to see what you are working towards. You will see the layout of the test papers and learn how to use the answer sheets. Don't worry if you find it hard at first, the *11+ Explained* will help you develop your skills.

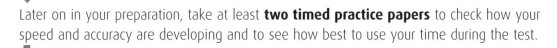

Later on in your preparation, take at least **two timed practice papers** to check how your speed and accuracy are developing and to see how best to use your time during the test.

Take a **timed practice paper a few days before the test** as final preparation.

Tips for using practice papers

- After learning about all of the question types, start taking timed practice papers to try out your test technique and to build your confidence in answering different question types. This will also help you switch quickly between different question types – a skill you will need in the test.
- After each practice paper, look at how you did in the test and decide what areas you need to work on before trying another practice paper.
- Leave at least 2 to 3 days between practice papers because that gives you time to work on your test technique. Taking practice papers too close together would be very tiring.
- When you get used to doing practice papers, ask your parent or carer to 'administer' the practice papers to make it more like the real test.

PARENT TIP   Which practice papers should we use?

We recommend that you use the GL Assessment *Official 11+ Practice Papers* series. As GL Assessment also develops the majority of actual 11+ tests, these will give you the most authentic practice available for the 11+ test, mirroring the exact design and approach of the real tests your child is likely to take. GL Assessment publishes two packs of practice papers for each subject (each with four tests). This should provide plenty of practice.

I'VE GONE THROUGH ALL THE QUESTION TYPES – WHAT SHOULD I DO NOW?

To do well in the 11+ test, you need to understand each question type and be confident that you can do the questions. Now you've worked through the question types, it's time to review your progress on each of the question types and see if there are any areas where you need more practice.

How can I check my progress?

> **Understanding question types + Confidence = Good performance**

As understanding the question types is so important, we'll start by showing you how to check your progress on each question type. This will help you work out what you need to do next, so that you get better scores next time.

Check your progress by asking yourself these questions for each question type:

> Check your **knowledge** of the question type. Ask yourself:
> - Do I understand what this question type is asking me to do?
> - Do I know the strategies I should use to answer this question type quickly and accurately?
>
> Then check your **confidence**. Ask yourself:
> - How happy do I feel about this question type?
> - Am I confident I can answer new questions of this type correctly?
>
> Finally, check your **performance** on the practice questions. Ask yourself:
> - Have I answered most of the practice questions correctly? (Use your Progress Chart to help you see how you've done on the practice questions.)

If you have mostly answered 'yes' to these questions, well done! You have learned the question type well and it's time to move on to develop your test technique. If you have answered 'no' to two or more of these questions, go back and review the question type. First check your knowledge and then build your confidence by trying the practice questions again.

It can be very useful for you to help your child review their progress. Although children can do this by themselves, working with another person may encourage them to think about it more carefully.

- Use the questions above, or similar ones, to encourage your child to reflect on their progress.
- Encourage your child to be realistic when assessing their knowledge, confidence and performance, getting them to think through their responses when necessary (for example, prompting them with questions like, 'Why do you think that?').
- You could begin by prompting your child to tell you how they think they are progressing. You might discuss issues, but they should make the final evaluation of their performance.
- Be positive and encouraging at all times, even when your child's knowledge and confidence are lower than they might want.

See also *The Official Parents' Guide to the 11+* (Chapter 11)

WHAT SHOULD I DO IN THE TIME LEFT BEFORE THE 11+ TEST?

As the 11+ test gets closer, you'll need to plan your time carefully. You are likely to be doing all the things shown in this diagram to get ready for the test.

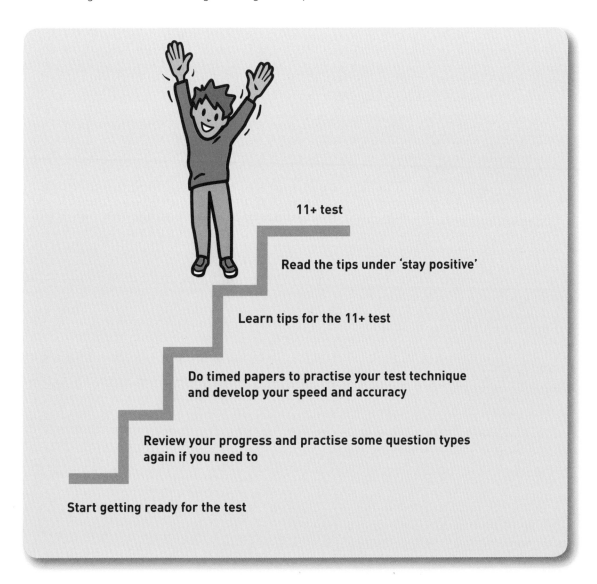

11+ test

Read the tips under 'stay positive'

Learn tips for the 11+ test

Do timed papers to practise your test technique and develop your speed and accuracy

Review your progress and practise some question types again if you need to

Start getting ready for the test

Find out some *tips for doing 11+ questions* on the next page

4 TIPS FOR DOING 11+ QUESTIONS

- HOW SHOULD I WORK OUT THE ANSWERS?
- WHAT IF I'M STUCK?
- IS IT OK TO CHANGE ANSWERS?
- HOW FAST DO I NEED TO WORK?
- HOW SHOULD I USE ANY TIME LEFT AT THE END?
- ANSWERING QUESTIONS
- ARE THERE ANY GENERAL RULES I CAN LEARN?

Here are some general tips and strategies that you can use in the 11+ test.

These tips will also be useful for other tests that you take in the future.

Most tests use a **multiple-choice format** where you have to pick the correct answer from a number of options you are given. Some tests use a **standard format** where you have to write your answer in the test booklet. We'll start by giving you tips that are the same for *both* multiple-choice and standard-format tests, and then we'll give you some tips for each of these formats.

HOW SHOULD I WORK OUT THE ANSWERS?

- Sometimes the answer to a question will seem obvious or 'jump off the page' at you. This can be good as it helps you answer the question quickly and gives you more time for other questions. But there is a danger that it could lead you to make mistakes.
- Try first to work out the answer from the information provided in the question, rather than looking immediately at the answer options, so you're sure why you've chosen a certain answer.
- Being able to explain the reasoning behind your answer will help you quickly check that your answer option is correct and give you confidence to move on to the next question.

WHAT IF I'M STUCK?

- It's easy to spend too long on a tricky question, especially if you're determined to get it right. But you'll lose time that you could spend on other questions that you might find easier.
- If you've tried using the tips and strategies you've learned, but still can't work out an answer, first try to narrow down some of the possible answers. You should be able to do this quickly, particularly if you use the strategies you've learned.
- Once you've ruled out any answers you're sure are wrong, think about the answer options you have left. It should now be much easier to answer the question correctly by making a 'best guess', based on the information that you know, rather than needing to make a wild guess.
- If you do make a 'best guess', note down the question number so you can go back and look at it again if you have time later.

IS IT OK TO CHANGE ANSWERS?

- Once you've chosen an answer, it's best not change it unless you have a good reason.
- Only change your answer if you're sure your first answer is wrong and you know the correct answer.

HOW FAST DO I NEED TO WORK?

- 11+ tests are timed and you may not manage to answer all the questions in the time available – many people don't. So you need to work at a fairly fast rate that allows you to try most of the questions, if not all of them. **It's possible you won't finish them all.**
- Try to set a pace that is comfortable, but still means you have to work hard, and stick to it. At points during the test you may want to pause to help you 'recharge' – relaxing and breathing deeply for a few seconds may help you.
- Try to answer as many questions as possible. If you run out of time, guess the remaining answers. You have a one-in-five chance of getting it right, but if you don't attempt the question, you have no chance of getting it right.
- Answering practice papers under timed conditions is the best way to find out how fast you need to work in the test.
- Remember to use a clock to help you when you do practice papers.

HOW SHOULD I USE ANY TIME LEFT AT THE END?

- It's important to work right up to when you're told to stop. Don't put your pen down just because you think you only have a few seconds left. Answering just one more question may make a difference!
- If you have any time left at the end of the test, check your answers! Don't stop working just because you've done all the questions.

ANSWERING QUESTIONS

- In multiple-choice tests it's easy to make mistakes moving from the question booklet to the answer sheet, so place the two as close together as you can.
- The print on the multiple-choice answer sheets is quite small, so be careful not to lose your place. Always check that the number on the answer sheet is the same as the number of the question you are answering in the question booklet.
- If you make a mistake, rub it out and put in your new answer. The multiple-choice tests will be marked by a machine. If you haven't rubbed out your first answer properly, the question will be marked wrong. Always use a pencil – never a pen.
- If you skip a question, remember to leave a space on your answer sheet. It's very easy to forget to do this in the actual test.
- For standard-format tests, make sure your answers are clear and legible, particularly if you have changed your answer.
- Don't be put off by a number of questions having the same answer option (for example, you have answered three 'C's in a row) – this does happen and doesn't automatically mean you have made a mistake.

As well as knowing how to solve each question type, it's also useful to learn some common rules for Non-Verbal Reasoning questions. If you find it tricky to work out an answer, you can then try using the rules to see if they help.

Remember, for some questions you may need to use two or even three of these rules together to get to the right answer. When you have found one rule, this may help you to eliminate answer options that are incorrect.

Questions can sometimes seem quite difficult when you first look at them. Don't panic! Work through the question carefully, bit by bit.

ARE THERE ANY GENERAL RULES I CAN LEARN?

- Sometimes it can be helpful to first look at the 'whole' question. You might immediately spot something that could be the solution. Then you can test this out first to save valuable time.
- Pick one feature at a time until you can rule out all the answer options except the right answer.

Count

- Count everything! Count the number of shapes, sides on a shape, parts of shapes that are shaded, types of shape (for example, black circles).
- Even count the number of straight lines for each shape and do the same for the curved lines.

Look at shapes

- If the shapes are the same, check that they are all the same size.
- Look at similar shapes to see what changes there are (for example, changes in size, colour, position, number of sides).
- Look at the outlines of shapes (for example, thin, thick, dashed, dotted, double lines). Are they the same or different?
- See if any shapes are 'cut-outs' or parts removed from other shapes.
- See if shapes are joined together, combined or split up. Do they overlap?

Look at shading and patterns

- Look at where and how shading is used. Check which way lines go if used for shading.
- Look for patterns in how shapes are arranged. Check for vertical, horizontal, clockwise or anti-clockwise arrangements. Do the patterns have to be symmetrical?

Look at position

- Check the direction of shapes (for example, are all arrows pointing in one direction or in a direction related to another shape?). Do they all face the same way?
- Check if shapes are rotated or reflected. Be careful not to confuse rotation and reflection. Turn the page around to see how the diagrams look when turned and to check for rotation.
- Shapes or parts of diagrams can be rotated in a clockwise or anti-clockwise direction. Carefully check that the angle of rotation is the same from diagram to diagram.
- Check the position of shapes in the diagram (for example, they are all on the left). Do they change position in a regular way (for example, they may move from inside to outside or from top to bottom)? Are they in a pattern?

Now try a *practice paper* to check your skills and try out these tips!

5 IMPROVING MY SPEED AND ACCURACY

- **HOW LONG IS THE 11+ TEST?**
- **WHY ARE SPEED AND ACCURACY SO IMPORTANT?**
- **HOW CAN I UNDERSTAND MORE ABOUT MY SPEED AND ACCURACY?**
- **HOW CAN I IMPROVE MY SPEED AND ACCURACY?**

HOW LONG IS THE 11+ TEST?

The 11+ test is timed. Each test you take will probably last between 40 and 50 minutes, but timings are different for each school as they use different tests.

You may not finish all the questions, but always try to answer as many as you can in the time you have. It's important to be as accurate as you can (that is, get as many questions right as you can and not make simple mistakes). You also have to work quickly so that you can have a go at most of the questions in the test. Remember:

> **Accuracy + Speed = A better test score**

The advice given here will help you improve your speed and accuracy. Your school may also give you some good advice on speed and accuracy.

PARENT TIP Are practice papers easier than the 11+ test?

In the 11+ test, questions may seem harder than in this book and in practice papers. We've used slightly easier questions in this book to help your child understand each question type and to build their confidence in being able to answer the questions correctly.

Questions may also seem harder in a test because your child will be working under a strict time limit. There are some tips below about how you can help your child to manage their time and how they can work through the questions as quickly and carefully as possible.

Most practice papers tend to be easier than the actual test. *The Official 11+ Practice Papers* contain more 'easy' or 'medium' difficulty questions than the real 11+ tests, and fewer 'difficult' items, to help children build up to the demands of the test. These practice papers offer the most authentic test preparation experience, as they cover the full range of question types used in the tests and draw on GL Assessment's long-standing specialist assessment expertise in constructing the real 11+ tests.

WHY ARE SPEED AND ACCURACY SO IMPORTANT?

In the 11+ test, you need to answer as many questions as you can without making careless mistakes. If you work too fast, you might get questions wrong that you should have got right. If you work carefully but too slowly, you might not answer enough questions – you need a balance of speed and accuracy.

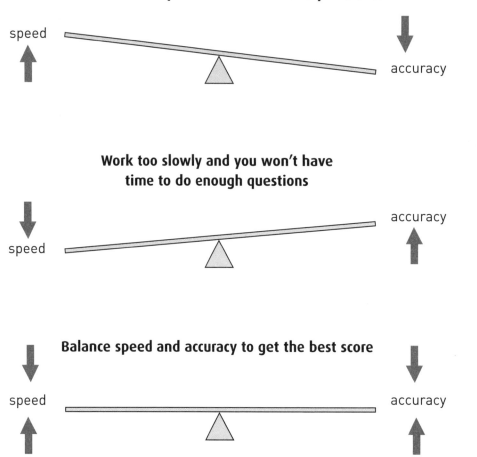

Work too fast and you'll make unnecessary mistakes

speed ↑   ↓ accuracy

Work too slowly and you won't have time to do enough questions

↓ speed   accuracy ↑

Balance speed and accuracy to get the best score

↓ speed   ↓ accuracy
↑   ↑

To improve your speed and accuracy, you need to know how you usually work. Do you work quickly, or more slowly and carefully? Even if you already have a good balance between speed and accuracy, you can still develop your test technique and improve your score.

HOW CAN I UNDERSTAND MORE ABOUT MY SPEED AND ACCURACY?

The best way to check how quickly and accurately you work is to do a timed practice paper. Then ask your parent or carer to help you work out and understand your scores, using the following tips:

- To find out **your speed**, count up how many questions you answered in the practice paper – it doesn't matter whether they are correct or not.
- Then find out **your score** on the practice paper by counting up the number of questions you answered correctly.
- To find out **your accuracy**, look at the difference between the number of questions you answered in total (your speed) and the number you answered correctly (your score).

You can use these numbers to help you think about your speed and accuracy like this:

- **Work on your accuracy** if there is a big difference between the total number of questions you have answered and the number of questions you got correct.
- **Work on your speed** if the total number of questions you have answered is much lower than the total number of questions in the test.

It takes time to develop speed and accuracy. You aren't expected to work both fast *and* accurately at first. Don't worry if, at first, you make mistakes on a practice paper. Find out where you went wrong so that you will be able to get a similar question right next time.

When you first do a practice paper, work slowly so you:

- make sure you use the tips and strategies that are right for each question type
- get used to changing between the different question types
- can build up your confidence for taking whole practice papers.

When you've got more used to doing practice papers and your test technique has developed, check your speed and accuracy again to see how you're improving. As you get close to the 11+ test, it's important that you get used to working both quickly and accurately.

PARENT TIP   **How can I best help my child with timed practice papers?**

You can help your child practise taking timed tests by acting as a 'test administrator', to create a more 'realistic' test situation:

- Make sure the practice paper is taken in an appropriate room – free from distractions and interruptions, not too hot or cold, etc.
- Time the test according to the instructions, providing a clear 'start' and 'stop' instruction.
- After the time is up, mark the test and discuss the score with your child.
- Ask your child to evaluate how they think they have done and explore their reasons for their response.

See also *The Official Parents' Guide to the 11+* (Chapter 12)

HOW CAN I IMPROVE MY SPEED AND ACCURACY?

- You need to practise doing timed 11+ practice papers.
- When you've finished a practice paper, check your speed and accuracy scores in the way described on page 20.
- Then look at the tips below to help you develop your test technique.

DEVELOPING YOUR ACCURACY

- Look back at Part 2 of the *11+ Explained* book to check you understand each question type properly.
- Check that you know the strategies for answering each question type.
- When you answer questions, try not to think about how much time is left, just concentrate on getting the answer right.
- Make sure you check each answer and are happy that it's correct before moving on to the next question.
- When you've improved your accuracy, you can develop your speed.

DEVELOPING YOUR SPEED

- Keep focused all the time during the test!
- Push yourself to work a bit faster than usual – this will become easier with practice.
- Check your answers quickly to make sure that you haven't made any careless mistakes, but move on as soon as you can.
- Make sure you know how long the 11+ test lasts and how many questions there are. Use this information to pace yourself, although you should leave slightly longer for questions towards the end of each section as these will tend to be more difficult.
- Make sure that you still work accurately, even though you're speeding up.
- You will usually be told when you have 5 minutes left. Make sure you use this time well and try to finish as many questions as you can.

When you feel ready, you may want to take another practice paper. Remember to use the skills you've been learning and practising. After finishing the practice paper, remember to check your speed and accuracy again to see what progress you have made.

22

Find out *how to deal with the 11+ challenge* on the next page!

6 DEALING WITH THE 11+ CHALLENGE

- WHY IS THE 11+ SUCH A CHALLENGE?
- HOW IMPORTANT IS THE 11+?
- HOW CAN MY EMOTIONS HELP ME?
- IS IT TIME FOR A REWARD?
- FACING THE CHALLENGE

WHY IS THE 11+ SUCH A CHALLENGE?

Preparing for the 11+ and doing the test can be hard work and can take a lot of time. You will probably find many questions quite hard, particularly when you first try them. The 11+ is designed to be challenging so it can work out people's different abilities. This means that even the most able people may find it hard sometimes.

With a challenge like the 11+ test, you'll probably feel many different emotions. Sometimes you might enjoy the challenge and feeling of achievement you get when you learn something new. Sometimes you might worry about the work you need to do or about your ability. This is perfectly natural. Here you can find out how to deal with these emotions.

HOW IMPORTANT IS THE 11+?

You're reading this book, so the 11+ is probably quite important to you and your family. Your 11+ results will affect your choice of school and your education for the next few years. So, the 11+ is important, but do remember these things:

The 11+ is only one part of everything that is going on in your life.	You may have to put off doing some things you enjoy for a short time, but don't stop doing everything you enjoy.	Preparing for the 11+ is a big commitment, but it will soon be over.
Although Non-Verbal Reasoning is an important ability, it is only one part of all your abilities.	**Stay positive and enjoy the challenge!**	
There are many things that the 11+ does not measure which you may be very good at.	In preparing for the 11+, you'll develop general skills that will be useful at school and later at work.	All you can expect of yourself is to do your best when preparing for the 11+.

As a parent, you will probably be the main influence on how your child sees the 11+ test. Your thoughts and feelings will be readily picked up by your child. If you feel positive about the experience, this will help your child feel more positive. If you're anxious, this may make your child more anxious.

It's perfectly natural to experience a wide range of emotions in relation to the 11+ test – both positive and negative. What's important is how you express these emotions and how you let them influence your behaviour. Remember:

- Put the 11+ test in perspective. Yes, it is important, but be careful not to let it take over your family's life.
- It is likely you will need to encourage and motivate your child to different degrees at different times. But don't put too much pressure on your child as this will raise their anxiety and have a negative effect on their 11+ preparation and test performance.
- Be aware of how you are feeling; accept your feelings as natural and find constructive ways of dealing with them (for example, by relaxing or exercising).
- Be conscious of how your feelings can affect your behaviour towards your child and make sure they don't have a negative effect (for example, getting frustrated with them about things to do with the 11+).
- Your feelings can affect both your verbal and non-verbal behaviour, so be aware both of what you're saying and how you're saying it or behaving.
- Use your own support network to help you deal with your feelings and concerns.

See also *The Official Parents' Guide to the 11+* (Chapter 11)

HOW CAN MY EMOTIONS HELP ME?

You will feel many different emotions because the 11+ is important to you. If you use them well, these emotions can help motivate you to do things, such as prepare for tests.

When you feel a strong emotion about the 11+ test, step back and ask yourself some questions:

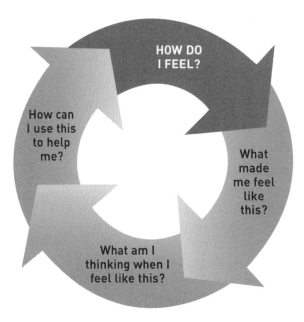

By answering these questions you will understand your emotions and see how they can help you. Sometimes it's useful to write down your answers to the questions, like in the following examples.

Here are two examples of how you can use these four steps to help you work through how you are feeling.

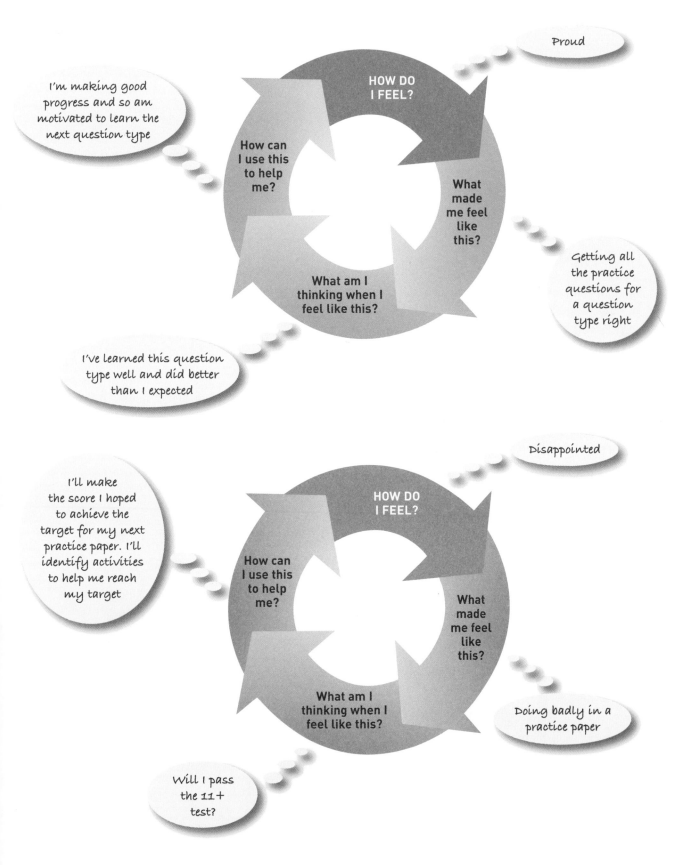

When you first do this activity it may be difficult to answer the questions, but it will become easier as you think more about your emotions.

Talk to your parents or carers about how you're feeling, too. They could go through the questions with you and help you decide what to do.

IS IT TIME FOR A REWARD?

Recognising your progress and effort is a great way of feeling positive about your preparation
and keeping motivated. Record your progress regularly on your timetable (see Chapter 2).
Make sure you use this and your Progress Chart to recognise your successes and help you
manage your time and activities.

Make sure you:
- Tick off every activity you do.
- Look back at your Progress Chart to see how much you have done and achieved.
- When you reach your 'success points', always reward yourself.
- Look ahead to see what you need to learn next and think about reaching your next success
  point.

FACING THE CHALLENGE

Lots of things can help us stay positive when we face a challenge such as the 11+. Often what we **do**, **think** and **feel** are connected, so *doing* something positive can help us *think* more positively and *feel* better.

DO

- When you're preparing for the 11+ test, stay focused and do your best. When you've finished, go and do something completely different.
- Eat well, sleep well and keep active.
- Be organised and prepared well in advance, so you don't have to rush round at the last minute to find things you need for the test.
- Don't talk too much to other children about the 11+ as this might make you nervous and wonder how you're doing compared to others. Everyone will have their own approach that works for them.

THINK

- It is all about doing the very best you can – think about this rather than competing too much with others.
- It can be easy for your thoughts about the 11+ to spill over into other areas of school and life (for example, 'I find the 11+ hard, so I'll find all tests hard'). Don't let this happen!
- It's normal to feel a range of emotions when facing a challenge like this. Use the questions on page 24 to understand your emotions and use them to help you.
- Be confident that you can tackle the test and do well. If there are things that you don't fully understand now, you can go back and learn them.

FEEL

- Be confident about your own ability and tell yourself things like 'I have prepared well' and 'I know how to do this question'.
- Sometimes you might feel emotions such as worry or fear. Remember that this is a natural reaction to any big event such as a test. Instead, try to think about how much you have achieved so far or do something that you enjoy to take your mind off the test.
- Try to find some time every day to relax and be calm. Do things that you enjoy, even if it is only for 10 minutes.
- Be proud of your achievements in working towards the 11+ and don't forget this, whatever your results.

Find out some *tips for the 11+ test* on the next page

On the day before the test	<ul><li>By now you will have done all you can to get ready for the test, so don't do any more last-minute practice or revision!</li><li>Get everything ready that you need for the test. Put it where you will remember to take it with you.</li><li>Do something relaxing or that you enjoy to take your mind off the test.</li><li>Get a good night's sleep – don't go to bed too late.</li></ul>
On the day of the test	<ul><li>Have a good breakfast with lots of 'energy' foods such as muesli, whole-grain cereal or porridge. Avoid 'heavy' foods that may make you feel tired, such as a cooked breakfast.</li><li>Wear comfortable clothes. It's a good idea to wear a number of layers in case you feel too hot or too cold.</li><li>Take everything you need for the test, particularly things like glasses or medication, plus any stationery that you are allowed to take in.</li><li>Leave plenty of time to get to the test centre. You don't want to be rushing and worrying about getting there on time.</li><li>Go to the toilet beforehand.</li><li>Try not to talk to others who are also taking the test before you go in – if they're nervous, they might make you nervous, too.</li></ul>
In the test	<ul><li>Listen carefully to the instructions that are read out. If you don't understand something, ask.</li><li>Read all the written instructions carefully and re-read them if you need to. This will help you avoid making mistakes.</li><li>Make sure you use the tips and strategies for each question type and the general test tips. If you can't do a question, try to rule out the answers you know are wrong and then make your 'best guess' from the answers left. If you note the question number, you can always come back to it at the end.</li><li>Focus on one question at a time and be positive about your ability to do well. Avoid thinking about how others are doing.</li><li>Keep calm and work steadily. Remember to check the time regularly, to make sure you know how long you have left.</li><li>Always use all of the time you have and never finish early.</li></ul>
After the test	<ul><li>You've finished! Getting this far is a great achievement, so be proud of yourself, whatever your results.</li><li>Now you've finished preparing for the 11+, use the spare time to catch up with your friends or enjoy your hobbies.</li><li>It will be some time before you find out your test results, so keep busy and try not to worry about them. Enjoy yourself!</li><li>Whatever the outcome of the 11+, you'll soon start a new school, so look forward to this new and exciting part of your life.</li></ul>

Good luck for the 11+ test!

Now go to Part 2 to find out about *Non-Verbal Reasoning question types*

PART 2

Non-Verbal Reasoning
question types explained

1 FINDING SIMILARITIES AND DIFFERENCES

The three question types in this section ask you to spot similarities and differences between diagrams. To do this you will need to draw on your powers of observation to see the small differences.

Use the step-by-step approach shown here and the tips for each question type to help you develop your skills.

QUESTION TYPES

FIND THE ODD ONE OUT

FIND THE DIAGRAM LIKE THE FIRST TWO

FIND THE DIAGRAM LIKE THE FIRST THREE

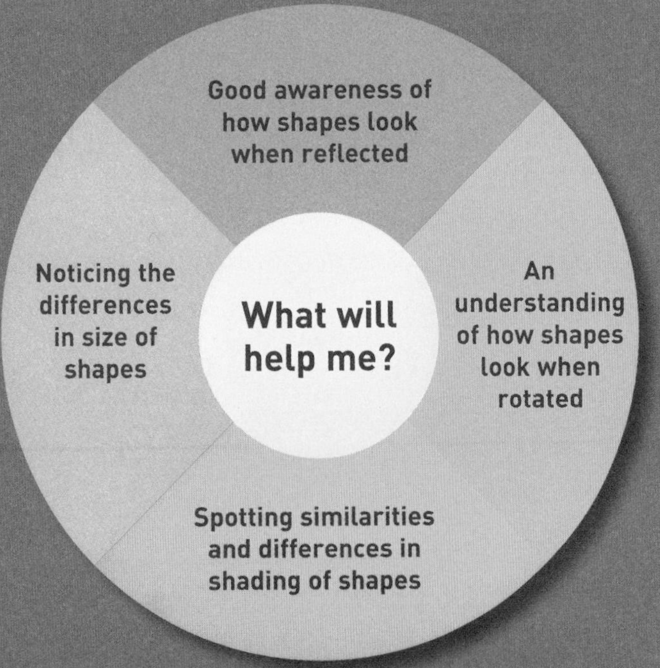

What will help me?

- Good awareness of how shapes look when reflected
- An understanding of how shapes look when rotated
- Spotting similarities and differences in shading of shapes
- Noticing the differences in size of shapes

3 STEPS TO SUCCESS

This 3-step method will help you solve all 11+ **FINDING SIMILARITIES AND DIFFERENCES** questions. It might seem a lot to do but, if you practise, you will soon be able to work through it quickly!

STEP 1 Identify one feature of the diagrams to look at first (for example, size of shape, shading, style of line). Compare this feature in all the diagrams. If this feature does not lead to the answer, move to Step 2.

STEP 2 Pick another feature and repeat Step 1. Do this with each feature, if needed.

STEP 3 If you've gone through all the obvious features and still can't find the answer, the rule you are looking for may be that two or more features are combined. (For example, you may have looked for a square in Step 1 and then at shading in Step 2, but the combination of the square and shading may be the important thing to look at.) Identify likely combinations and test these out using the first two steps.

Remember the features to look for!

Angles of rotation

Number of sides, shapes and lines

Size of shapes

Where small shapes or lines are positioned

Explore combinations of features and rules

Reflection

Shading

KEY WORDS

Diagram: describes a whole drawing. The word 'figure' is used in the 11+ test, but we think that 'diagram' is easier to understand while learning how to do the questions.

Shape: an individual shape, such as a square, hexagon, triangle or circle. A diagram can be made up of a single shape or a number of shapes.

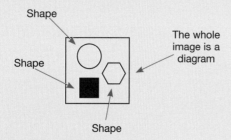

Shape

Shape

The whole image is a diagram

Shape

Shape

Rules and features: these are what make the difference, or similarity, or change between diagrams. For example, a square has four sides and a pentagon has five sides. In FIND THE ODD ONE OUT questions you may find four squares and one pentagon. Using the rule about number of sides means the pentagon will be the odd one out.

Counting: often you will need to count the number of sides of a shape or the number of objects inside a bigger shape.

Overlap: where shapes are on top of each other. They can either be in front of or behind the other.

Positioning of shapes: where shapes are placed. For example, they can be above, below or to the sides and at angles to each other.

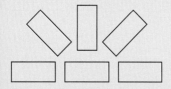

Reflection: where you can see a shape is the mirror image of another. Here the shape is reflected horizontally.

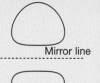

Mirror line

And here the shape is reflected vertically.

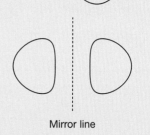

Mirror line

Rotation: where shapes are turned round. The angle of rotation tells you how the shapes have been rotated, for example by 45° each time here.

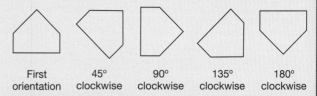

| First orientation | 45° clockwise | 90° clockwise | 135° clockwise | 180° clockwise |

Shading: how shapes are filled. Here you can see the shapes are filled with a solid shade, lines and then dots. Other shading may also be used, such as crosses or stars.

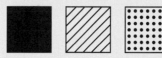

Symmetry: a line of symmetry through a shape is the line on which you could fold the shape perfectly in half. If it is a regular shape, then the number of lines of symmetry equals the number of sides. Some shapes have no lines of symmetry.

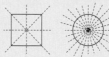

| 4 lines of symmetry | An infinite number of lines of symmetry | 1 line of symmetry | No lines of symmetry | 5 lines of symmetry |

FIND THE ODD ONE OUT

In these questions, you are shown five diagrams. You have to find the one that is different in some way from the other four.

You need to be good at quickly spotting similarities and differences between diagrams to find the odd one out. Sometimes these will be easy to see straight away. Other times you will have to spend some time working out the rules that make four diagrams the same and one different.

Example
Which is the odd one out here?

Answer
Of course, you know that the duck is the odd one out because it is not a fish. In this case, you know automatically what the differences are between fish and ducks – a duck doesn't live completely in the water, even though it can swim very well. Of course, there are lots of other features and rules that make ducks and fish different. For example, a duck is the only one that has feathers. Try to think of three more differences.

In this question type, there will be rules that make things the same as and different from each other, but you will have to try a bit harder to work out the rules!

11+ STYLE QUESTION

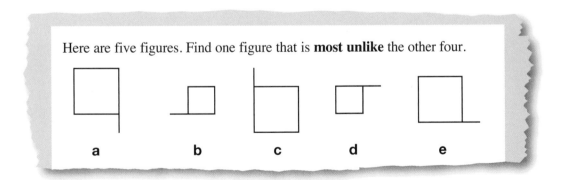

Here are five figures. Find one figure that is **most unlike** the other four.

a   b   c   d   e

HOW TO DO IT

  Follow the **3 steps to success** (from page 31) to work out the answer. For easy questions you may only need to use two of the steps, but for more difficult questions you may need to use all three steps.

TIP ....
If this feature appears in more than one diagram, it probably won't lead you to the correct answer, because only *one* of the diagrams can be the odd one out. For example, if all the shapes are the same size, then size cannot be the rule you are looking for.

① Pick out one main feature of the diagrams to look at first. Let's start with the size of the square shape in each diagram. Is it the same size in more than one diagram? As two of the shapes are small and three are big, difference in size doesn't make any *one* diagram the odd one out.

② So choose another feature to look at. The other obvious feature is the short line sticking out from one corner of each shape. Are all these lines the same? They are all the same length, but are they all in exactly the same position?

Look at diagram **a**. The short line falls from the bottom right corner of the square. Now look at diagram **b** and turn the page round, so that the line is at the bottom of the square. Now you can see if the line falls from the bottom right corner of this square, too. Do the same for each of the answer options.

TIP ....
Remember to look out for how features may be combined.

You will notice that diagram **e** is different from the rest, as the line falls from the bottom left corner of the square when you turn the page round. Therefore diagram **e** must be the odd one out.

Answer e

A MORE DIFFICULT QUESTION

Use the **3 steps to success** with this more difficult question to quickly find the odd one out.

PARENT TIP ....
Many puzzles are based on skills of logic, observation and spatial ability and so will help your child develop their Non-Verbal Reasoning skills. Buy your child a puzzle book, perhaps as a small reward for their hard work. Look out for 'spot the difference', 'odd one out' and 'mazes' puzzles.

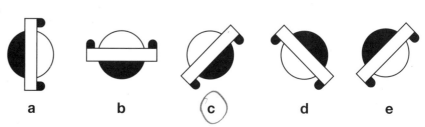

a   b   c   d   e

① Look at the size of the whole diagrams. Are they all the same size? Yes. Are each of the elements (large circle, long thin rectangle, small semi-circles) within the diagrams the same size? Yes.

② As size has nothing to do with the solution, choose another feature and repeat Step 1. Let's pick the white rectangle that appears across the centre of diagram **a**. In Step 1 we decided that these were all the same size. But does the white rectangle appear in the centre of each diagram? Yes. As both features we've looked at are the same in at least two of the diagrams, we have to choose another feature to think about. There are two small semi-circular arches, one at each end of the rectangle. Does every diagram have them? Yes.

TIP ....
Remember **ANSWERS**. Look out for mirrored shapes and different styles of lines, such as thick, thin, dotted or dashed.

Small semi-circular arches

Large circle

Thin rectangle

TIP

Watch out for where shapes appear inside other shapes, overlap with other shapes or are outside or attached to other shapes. Shapes can also be moved around.

3 We've been through all the obvious features now, but still haven't found the answer. Maybe some rules are being used together. All the diagrams have the small semi-circular arches, but now check their position, too. What do you notice? The semi-circular arches are only on the same side as the black side of the big circle in diagram **c**, so **c** must be the odd one out.

Answer c

> There may be some parts of the diagram that you can sometimes ignore. The shading might change in each diagram, but it might not have anything to do with finding the odd one out.

Katy

YOUR TURN

In each of the rows below there are five figures. Find one figure in each row that is **most unlike** the other four. Circle its letter.

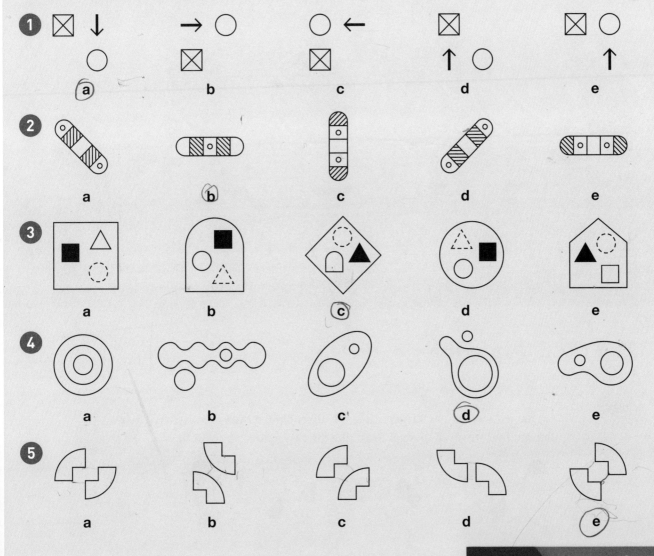

FIND THE DIAGRAM LIKE THE FIRST TWO

In these questions, you are shown two diagrams that are alike in one or more ways. You need to look for similarities between the two diagrams and work out which of five answer options goes with them best.

You will need to be good at spotting similarities and differences for these questions and so the work that you have already done on FIND THE ODD ONE OUT will help you. You also need to have an eye for detail and know how to work out rules.

You will be able to use the same approach with the next question type – FIND THE DIAGRAM LIKE THE FIRST THREE.

Example
Here are an apple and some grapes.

Which of the following five fruits most closely belongs with the apple and grape?

Answer
The pear belongs with them because you can eat its skin, too. You might have thought the answer was the lime because it's green and so are apples and some grapes. But watch out! A pear is also green so, if you used the rule 'they are all green', you would have had two possible answers – lime and pear.

11+ STYLE QUESTION

On the left there are two figures that are alike. On the right there are five more figures: find which of these is **most like** the two figures on the left.

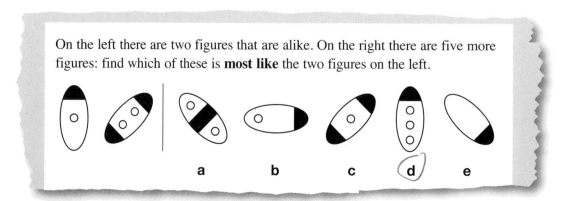

a   b   c   d   e

HOW TO DO IT

Follow the **3 steps to success** to work out the answer. For easy questions you may only need to use two of the steps, but for more difficult questions you may need to use all three steps.

1 Look at the two diagrams before the line. The question tells us that they must be alike in some way and so first we have to work out what they have in common. After that, we have to look for similarities with the answer options.

TIP..........................
Remember **ANSWERS**. You may need to look for lines of symmetry or the position of shapes.

Notice that the main shape in both of the diagrams before the line is an oval or ellipse. All the answer options also have an oval, so this alone is not the answer.

2 Look at the other features. The first oval has one circle inside it and one end shaded. The second has two circles inside it and two ends shaded.

3 So now we know the rule is that the diagram must be an oval with an equal number of circles and ends shaded.

Only answer option **b** fits the rule we have spotted and so must be the correct answer.

Answer b

A MORE DIFFICULT QUESTION

Use the **3 steps to success** with this more difficult question to quickly find out which diagram is like the first two.

PARENT TIP..................
Children must spot what different diagrams have in common to be able to do this question type. Get your child to think about similarities and differences between things. For example, name an object. Then ask your child to quickly think of other objects that are either like it or different from it in some way and to explain why.

Remember, the two diagrams on the left of the line are alike in some way. Which diagram on the right of the line is **most like** the two diagrams on the left?

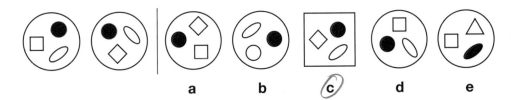

a   b   c   d   e

TIP..........................
If a feature you're looking at does not appear in any of the five answer options, then you can ignore it.

1 Look at the large circle surrounding the smaller shapes in the group of two diagrams. Is this the same in more than one answer option? Four of the answer options have the same large circle but **c** is different as it has a large square, so we can eliminate **c** as a possible answer. Now we also know that the large circle alone isn't going to be the reason for the answer.

2 So, choose another feature and repeat Step 1. Both diagrams on the left have a small black circle inside the large circle. We can now eliminate **e** as a possible solution, as it does not contain a black circle. That leaves **a**, **b** and **d** as possible answers.

3 Look at the other small shapes to see if they are the same in both diagrams on the left. Both have a small unshaded square. So do answer options **a** and **d**. This rules out **b** as a possible answer. Both diagrams on the left also have a small unshaded oval.

Only diagram **d** meets all the rules of the first two diagrams. It has the same large shape and the same small shapes with the same shading inside.

Answer d

YOUR TURN

On the left of each of the rows below there are two figures that are alike. On the right there are five more figures: find which of these is **most like** the two figures on the left. Circle its letter.

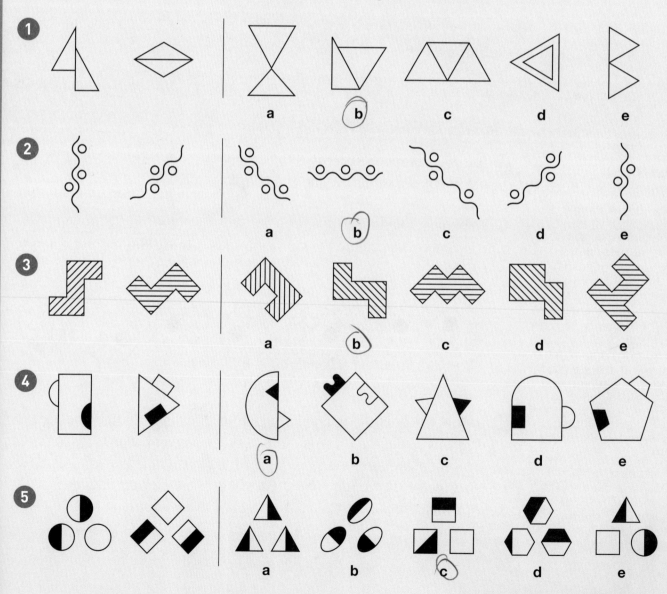

Answers   Progress Chart

FIND THE DIAGRAM LIKE THE FIRST THREE

In these questions, you are shown three diagrams that are alike in one or more ways. You need to look for similarities between the three diagrams on the left and work out which of the five answer options goes with them best.

Remember, you can do this question in the same way as FIND THE DIAGRAM LIKE THE FIRST TWO. So you will need to be good at spotting similarities and differences. You must also look carefully at the details in the diagrams, so that you can work out the rules for finding what is the same about the diagrams.

Example
Here are some pictures.

Which of the following vehicles belongs most closely with them?

Answer
The bus belongs with them because it also has four wheels. You might have thought that the answer was lorry because you can get inside it, as you can in the car and van. But you can't get inside the tractor, so 'getting inside it' isn't the link between the car, the tractor and the van.

11+ STYLE QUESTION

On the left there are three figures that are alike. On the right there are five more figures: find which of these is **most like** the three figures on the left.

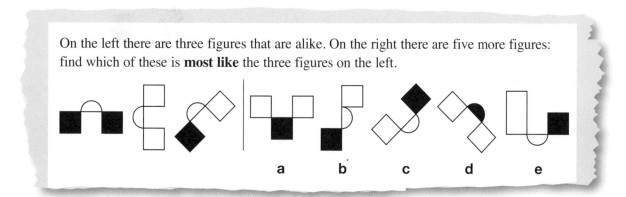

HOW TO DO IT

TIP

If the feature you chose does not appear in any diagram in the answer options, then you can eliminate it. For example, maybe you picked the angle of the diagram as the first feature to look at. As all the diagrams are placed at different angles, you can rule this out.

TIP

If you've gone through each feature in turn and still can't find the answer, try combining some of the rules and then try them out. For example, here you needed to notice that all the diagrams had squares linked by a semi-circle. But you also had to spot that the squares were both on the same side of the line and were opposite the semi-circle.

Follow the **3 steps to success** to work out the answer. For easy questions you may only need to use two of the steps, but for more difficult questions you may need to use all three steps.

1 To answer this question, you need to find out what the three diagrams before the line have in common and what similarities they have with the answer options. Which of the five answer options fits best with the group of three on the left?

It's easy to see that each of the three diagrams on the left has two squares linked by a white semi-circle. To be like them, this means that the correct answer must follow this rule, too. So we can rule out answer options **a**, **d** and **e** straight away. We will have to find another link between the first three diagrams, so that we can choose between the answer options that are left – **b** and **c**.

2 Is it the shading of the squares that makes the diagrams on the left the same? This shading seems to be quite random – either none, one or both of the squares are shaded. It's not the feature that makes them similar.

Look at the position of these squares. In the first three diagrams, they're all on the opposite side of the line to the semi-circle. So the only answer option matching all the rules is **c**.

Answer c

A MORE DIFFICULT QUESTION

Use the **3 steps to success** with this more difficult question to quickly find out which diagram is like the first three.

Remember, the three diagrams on the left of the line are alike in some way. Which one of the diagrams to the right of the line is **most like** the three diagrams on the left?

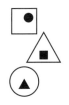 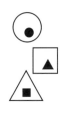 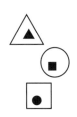 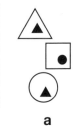 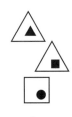 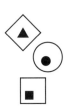  

                                      a   **b**   **c**   **d**   **e**

1 Try size of shape. Are all the larger shapes in each of the three diagrams to the left of the line the same size? How about the smaller black shapes inside the larger ones? As they are all the same size, size probably isn't a solution.

TIP
Similarities and differences can be made by different numbers of shapes or shapes can be combined with each other. Sometimes different numbers of shapes or parts of shapes are shaded.

TIP
Remember **ANSWERS**. You might need to spot several features at once.

2 So choose another feature. All the diagrams in the group of three have three larger shapes and three smaller shapes, each contained inside the larger shapes. Also, all have a square, a circle and a triangle as their large shapes, even though they are in a different order. Answer options **b** and **c** don't fit this rule, so can't be the right answer. This leaves **a**, **d** and **e** as possible answers.

3 Look at the small black shapes. Again, in the group of three, each diagram has the same three small shapes, even though they are in a different order. If you look through the answer options, you can see that only **e** matches the group of three, so it must be the right answer.

Sometimes the lines that are shading a shape go in different directions.

Anita

Answer e

YOUR TURN

On the left of each of the rows below there are three figures that are alike. On the right there are five more figures: find which of these is **most like** the three figures on the left. Circle its letter.

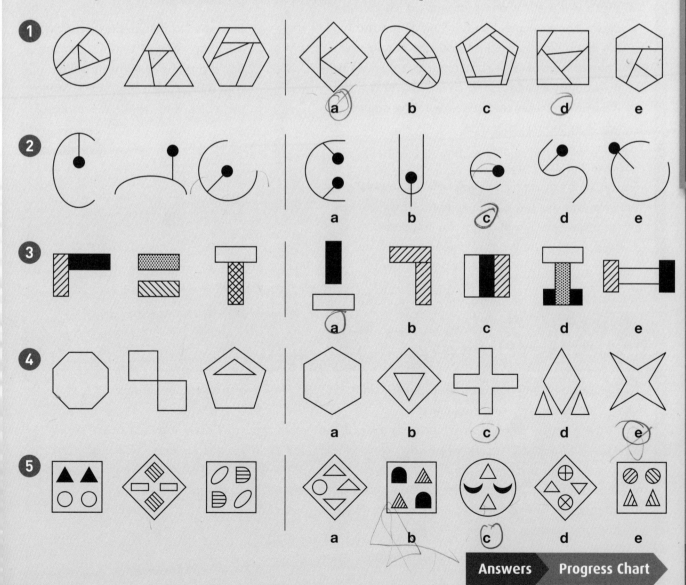

non-verbal fun

Object chains

This game will help you think about the features of objects and how these are similar and different from the features of other objects. Play it with a family member or friend.

● Make a 'chain' of objects by thinking about what features two objects share. Players take it in turns to add a new object to the chain.

● The first player starts by saying, 'I'm thinking of a ...' and adds an object to the end. For example, 'I'm thinking of a car'.

● The second player then chooses an object that's like the first player's and says why. For example, 'I'm thinking of a bicycle. It's like a car because it has wheels'.

● The next player then chooses another object that's like the last one that was added to the chain. For example, 'I'm thinking of scooter. It's like a bicycle because you ride it'.

● Take it in turns until someone can't think of a new object to add to the chain. Or set a time limit of 4 minutes and see how many objects you can chain in this time.

Increase the challenge!
Try chaining objects using two shared features. For example, 'I'm thinking of a telephone'. Then the next player might say, 'I'm thinking of a computer. It's like a telephone because it has a keypad and you can use it to communicate with people'.

Quickfire questions

These quickfire questions will start you thinking about similarities and differences and links between things, just like the 11+ questions do.

1 Which letter is the odd one out? Why? **A M N U V**

2 Find one of each of the following coins: 1p, 2p, 5p, 10p and 50p. Line them up next to each other. Which could be the odd one out?

3 Now do the same with 2p, 5p, 10p, 20p and 50p coins. Which is the odd one out? What are two possible answers?

4 Find the following coins: 1p, 2p, 5p, 10p, 20p, 50p, £1 and £2. Put the 5p, 20p and 50p coins in a line together. Which one of the other five coins is most like these three?

Answers

Spot the difference

This quick game will help you look out for tiny changes. Play it with a family member or friend when you have a few spare minutes.

■ Draw a simple picture on a piece of paper, for example a person. Give it to the other player.

■ They add a small feature while you aren't looking, for example one eyebrow. Then you have to spot what they have done.

■ You could also play this with a picture cut out of a magazine. Look at the picture for 30 seconds first to memorise the details. Then the other player alters it in a small way and you have to spot the difference.

2 COMPLETING DIAGRAMS

These question types involve working out the links between diagrams. You will need to be good at comparing diagrams to spot changes from one diagram to another. You will then need detective skills to work out how the rule for that change can be used on another diagram.

The careful step-by-step approach shown here will help. Use the tips to help you develop your skills. Work on one question type will help you with the other question types.

QUESTION TYPES

COMPLETE THE SERIES

COMPLETE THE GRID

COMPLETE THE PAIR

Spotting differences in size of shapes

Spotting similarities and differences in shading

Good awareness of how shapes look when rotated or reflected

What will help me?

Noticing how shapes combine to create new shapes

Being able to combine rules to work out more complex diagrams

3 STEPS TO SUCCESS

This 3-step method will help you solve most 11+ **COMPLETING DIAGRAMS** questions. It might seem a lot to do but, if you practise it, you will soon be able to work through it quickly!

STEP 1   Pick one feature that stands out to you from the first diagram. Decide whether it changes from diagram to diagram and how it changes. Is there a pattern?

STEP 2   If you can see the rule for this feature and can work out how it should look in the missing diagram, check the answer options to see if this might be the correct answer. If you notice that other changes are also taking place from diagram to diagram, repeat Step 1 with another feature. Eliminate incorrect answer options as you go.

STEP 3   If you've worked through all the features in turn and still can't find the answer, think about how two or more changes might be combined. For example, only certain parts of shapes might be shaded and the shading might change direction, or shapes might swap places and sizes. Identify likely combinations of changes to features and test these out using the two steps above. You will now have found the rules for the changes and will be able to work out the answer.

A
N
S
W
E
R
S

Remember the features to look for!

Angles of rotation

Number of sides, shapes and lines

Size of shapes

Where small shapes or lines are positioned

Explore combinations of features and rules

Reflection

Shading

KEY WORDS

Diagram: describes a whole drawing. In these question types, a 'box' either contains a diagram or is empty. The words 'figure' and 'square' are used in the 11+ test, but we think that 'diagram' and 'box' are easier to understand while learning how to do the questions.

Shape: an individual shape, such as a square, hexagon, triangle or circle. A diagram can be made up of a single shape or a number of shapes.

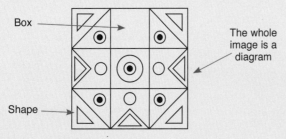

Box

The whole image is a diagram

Shape

Rules and features: these are what make the difference, similarity, change or progression between diagrams. For example, a large circle may contain one small triangle in the first box and then two triangles in the second box and three triangles in the third. Here the rule is 'one more small triangle inside the large circle for each box in turn'.

Counting: often you will need to count the number of sides of a shape or the number of objects inside a bigger shape.

Overlap: where shapes are on top of each other. They can either be in front of or behind the other.

Positioning of shapes: where shapes are placed. For example, they can be above, below or to the sides and at angles to each other.

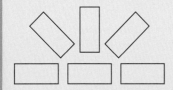

Reflection: where you can see a shape is the mirror image of another. Here the shape is reflected horizontally.

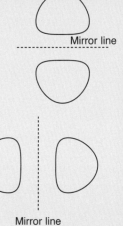

Mirror line

And here the shape is reflected vertically.

Mirror line

Rotation: where shapes are turned round. The angle of rotation tells you how the shapes have been rotated, for example by 45° each time here.

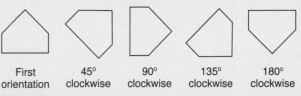

| First orientation | 45° clockwise | 90° clockwise | 135° clockwise | 180° clockwise |

Shading: how shapes are filled. Here you can see the shapes are filled with a solid shade, lines and then dots. Other shading may also be used, such as crosses or stars.

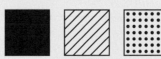

Symmetry: a line of symmetry through a shape is the line on which you could fold the shape perfectly in half. If it is a regular shape, then the number of lines of symmetry equals the number of sides. Some shapes have no lines of symmetry.

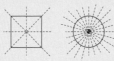

4 lines of symmetry • An infinite number of lines of symmetry • 1 line of symmetry • No lines of symmetry • 5 lines of symmetry

COMPLETE THE SERIES

In these questions, you are given five boxes in a line (called 'squares' in the 11+ test). One of these boxes does not contain a diagram. You have to decide which of the answer options fills the empty box.

The easiest way to work out the answer to this question type is to follow the step-by-step approach given. For easy questions you might only need to use one or two steps, but for more difficult questions you might need to work through all three steps.

There are many variations for this question type, as you will see when you start trying some of the 11+ questions. Sometimes there is a regular change of a feature in the diagram from box to box. In other questions, there is a different diagram in each box, to make a pattern across the boxes.

Example
Which stamp should you buy to go with these?

Which one?

Answer
If you chose the correct stamp, you will notice a pattern. The face has changed from box to box – the head has rotated all the way round!

11+ STYLE QUESTION

To the left there are five squares arranged in order. One of these squares has been left empty. Find which one of the five squares on the right should **take the place** of the empty square.

                                            a   b   c   d   e

HOW TO DO IT

TIP..........................
Sometimes the first or second box might be empty. If so, it can help to work backwards along the row of five boxes.

Follow the **3 steps to success** (from page 43) to work out the answer. For easy questions you may only need to use two of the steps, but for more difficult questions you may need to use all three steps.

1 Identify one feature from the first box to start with. Look at the position of the small black square in each box. If you follow it, you can see that it moves down bit by bit in each diagram until it's at the bottom of the last box.

Where should the small black square go in the empty box? Looking at the pattern, we can see that it should be positioned in the centre of the box. This means that **a**, **c** and **d** are possible answers. **b** and **e** cannot be right, so eliminate them.

TIP..........................
Remember **ANSWERS**. Many of the changes to the features will be to do with rotation and counting. Or features might be left out or change shading.

2 Now look at the hexagon with the top side missing from it in the first box. What happens to the hexagon from box to box? A side disappears in each box, going in a clockwise direction around the hexagon. Look at this pattern to identify how complete the hexagon should be in the empty box.

TIP..........................
Sometimes you have to find out several rules. This can make the questions seem more challenging. But pick one feature at a time and keep repeating Steps 1 and 2 until you can rule out all the answer options except the right answer.

3 We have now looked at both shapes that appear in the boxes – the hexagon and the square. They are the same shade and size in each box. This means that we can combine the rules about the position of the square and the sides of the hexagon to find the answer. Nothing else changes. Only option **d** has the sides of the hexagon and the small square in the right place.

Answer d

VARIATIONS

Not all **COMPLETE THE SERIES** questions will have a small change from box to box like you saw in the 11+ question above. Sometimes the whole box changes, making a pattern across the boxes. Look at how the correct answer is worked out in this example and you will be able to follow this approach if you come across variations like it. You probably won't need to follow all three steps to find the answer to questions like this.

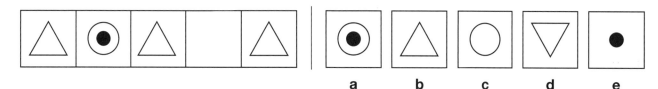

In this example, look at every other box. Can you see a pattern? Do you know what should go in the empty box? Here the rule is triangles go in every other box. This means that the circles will also be in alternate boxes, so answer option **a** is the correct answer.

Answer a

PARENT TIP

Doing jigsaws and Sudoku puzzles with your child will help you build Non-Verbal Reasoning skills together and they can be fun to do!

Check for any alternating patterns. If there aren't any then work out what changes as you move from one diagram to the next.

Sian

YOUR TURN

To the left in each of the lines below there are five squares arranged in order. One of these squares has been left empty. Find which one of the five squares on the right should **take the place** of the empty square. Circle its letter.

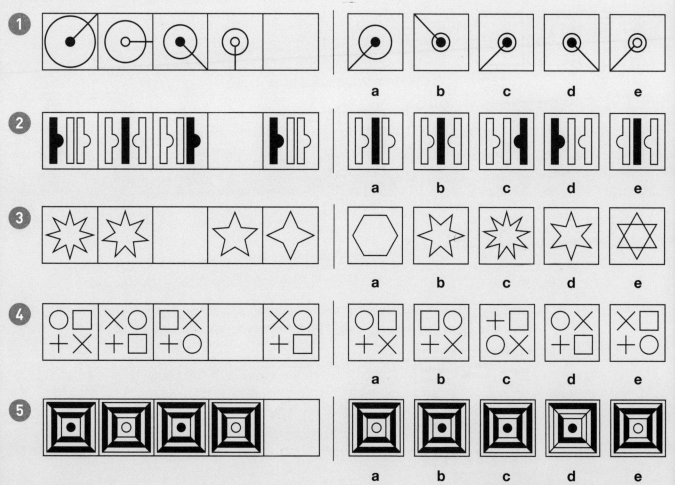

COMPLETE THE GRID

COMPLETE THE GRID questions are just that! You have to find out which of the answer options fits the empty box in the grid. There are two styles of grids in these questions:

2 x 2

3 x 3

For all these questions you must be able to work through the features of each diagram (called 'figures' in the 11+ test) step by step, spotting similarities, changes and patterns.

Example
Imagine these are some bathroom tiles. Draw the tile that completes the grid.

Answer
Did you spot the pattern of the tiles? In this case, the *number* of shells changed from tile to tile *and* all tiles together made a symmetrical pattern.

11+ STYLE QUESTION

In the big square on the left below one of the small squares has been left empty. One of the five figures on the right should fill the empty square. Find this figure.

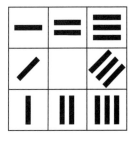

a   b   c   d   e

HOW TO DO IT

Follow the **3 steps to success** to work out the answer. For easy questions you may only need to use two of the steps, but for more difficult questions you may need to use all three steps.

1 One of the first things you need to decide is whether the pattern made by the diagrams is arranged in rows, columns or both. Looking at the complete rows and columns (those without the missing diagram) will help. A quick glance might give you a clue as to whether you need to work in rows or columns, but sometimes you will need to study the diagrams more carefully to spot this. When you have decided, pick one feature of the diagrams to look at first.

TIP

Decide whether you need to work with rows or columns, or both rows and columns. Sometimes there will be an overall pattern instead.

What happens to the black rectangle? We need to work out how it relates to the black rectangle in the boxes next to it. The black rectangle in the top row becomes two rectangles and then three across the row. Checking the columns tells us that we must have two rectangles in the empty box.

TIP

Remember **ANSWERS**. Many of the changes to the features will be to do with rotation and counting. Features might be left out, or move around or swap shading.

2 But the number of rectangles isn't all that changes. The position of the rectangles changes down the column, but across the row they are all lined up in the same direction.

3 We can see that the other complete row seems to follow the same rules, too. Therefore, to fill in the empty box, we're looking for an answer option containing two rectangles that are slanted in the same direction as the others in the middle row. So we can eliminate answer options **c** and **d** straight away because they don't have the right shape or the right number of shapes.

The only answer option left that fits our rules of two black rectangles facing the *same* direction as the rest of the row is **a**.

Answer a

VARIATIONS

These questions can have many different variations. They are likely to be similar to the ones shown on the next page. Look at how the correct answer is worked out in these examples and you will be able to follow this approach if you come across variations like these.

Complete the 2 x 2 grid

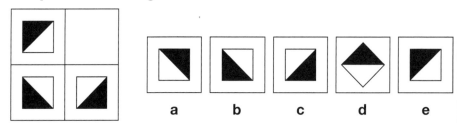

In each of the boxes the shaded half of the square is next to the outer corner of the grid. So **a** must be the answer.

Complete the 3 x 3 grid – rows

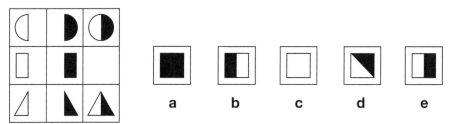

Can you see that the pattern in this grid goes across the rows? So the key is to look at the rows to work out the answer. The diagrams in the first two boxes in a row combine to form the shape in the third box in the row. So the answer here must be **e**.

Complete the 3 x 3 grid – columns

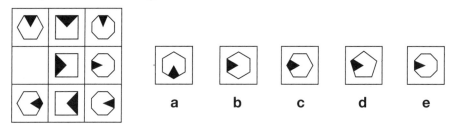

In this example, the pattern goes down the columns. The large shape in each box is the same in each column and the shaded part moves from the top to the left and then to the right side of the shape. Now we have to use the rules that we worked out for the two complete columns to find the empty box in the other column. Answer option **c** is the only one that fits the rules we worked out for the other two columns.

Sometimes the grid is like a jigsaw and it's like looking for a missing piece.

Gary

Complete the 3 x 3 grid – patterns

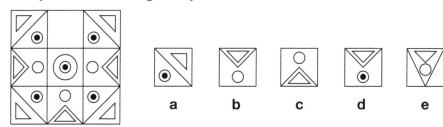

Here the whole grid has been divided into a pattern. Each box contains a part of the overall pattern. In this example the empty box must be the same as the centre cells in the first and third columns and the centre of the bottom row, but rotated to make the pattern perfect. Only answer option **b** completes the pattern properly.

Complete the 3 x 3 grid – arranging the shapes

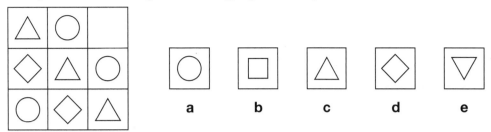

This grid has three sets of shapes and is sometimes called a 'Latin square'. (A Latin square is a grid where each symbol occurs once in each row and once in each column.) Count the number of shapes in each row and each column. Do you notice that each shape appears once in each row and once in each column? So a diamond is missing and only answer option **d** can be correct. Sometimes the position or number of the shapes will be important, too. Any shapes can be used in Latin squares.

YOUR TURN

In the big square on the left of each line below one of the small squares has been left empty. One of the five figures on the right should fill the empty square. Find this figure each time. Circle its letter.

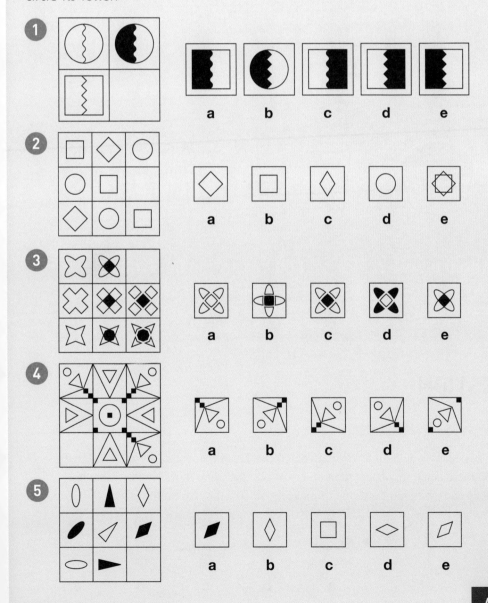

COMPLETE THE PAIR

In these questions, you are shown a pair of diagrams. You must first work out how they go together. Then you have to choose which one of the five answer options goes with the third diagram to make another pair of diagrams that are related in the same way as the first two.

You will have to work out what changes take place from the first diagram to the second diagram and the rules that make them a pair. For this, you will need to be good at spotting small changes and finding out rules so, again, your detective skills will be useful.

Think about how things go together in real life to make pairs:

These things aren't exactly the same, but we know they go together and we can explain why. In these questions, you need to find reasons why diagrams go together, but the reasons probably won't be so obvious straight away.

Example
Decide why the cakes are a pair. Then decide which beaker is needed to make a pair of beakers.

Answer
The pink beaker without a straw. The second cake case becomes the colour of the first sweet, and the sweet disappears! The correct beaker becomes the colour of the first straw, and the straw disappears.

11+ STYLE QUESTION

On the left below are two shapes with an arrow between them. Decide how the second is related to the first. After these there is a third shape, then an arrow and then five more shapes. Decide which of the five shapes goes with the third one to make a pair like the two on the left.

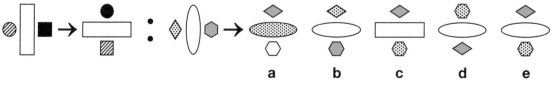

HOW TO DO IT

COMPLETE THE PAIR

Follow the **3 steps to success** to work out the answer. For easy questions you may only need to use two of the steps, but for more difficult questions you may need to use all three steps.

TIP..........................
Look at the first pair of diagrams together. Does one obvious change stand out, such as rotation, reflection, position or size? Is this the only change taking place or is there more going on?

1 To start off, try to work out the rules for what changes take place from the first diagram to the second. Look closely at features of the shapes that make up these two diagrams. Count the shapes, look at their sizes and look at their shading. Did you notice that there is the same number of shapes in each diagram here and that they are also the same size? So what's changed?

2 The whole diagram has been rotated 90° clockwise.

3 But that's not all. The small shapes have also swapped shading, while the big rectangle stays the same.

TIP..........................
Remember **ANSWERS**. Many of the changes to the features will be to do with rotation and counting. Features might be left out, or move around or change shading.

Use these rules to decide which answer option goes with the third diagram to make a pair in the same way. Look for the same changes. Here the correct answer option must have the same shapes, in the same sizes. So you can eliminate **c**. The diagram must be turned on its side, so that the small diamond will be above the oval and the shading of only the small shapes must swap. Only **e** does all this.

Answer e

A MORE DIFFICULT QUESTION

Use the **3 steps to success** to solve a more difficult question.

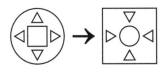 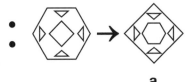 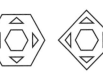

                                                  a   b   c   d   e

TIP..........................
Watch out for size and position of shapes changing from the first diagram in the pair to the second.

1 You can see by looking at the diagram as a whole that more than one change takes place from the first diagram to the second diagram in the pair. There's probably too much going on for you to discover an obvious rule immediately. So, begin by looking at the features of the first pair of diagrams one at a time. The basic shapes that make up the diagrams seem a good place to start.

An immediate feature of the first diagram is the large circle around all the small shapes. What changes take place to the circle? It's smaller and placed at the centre of the second diagram. What happens to the square at the centre of the first diagram? It gets bigger and is put around all the small shapes.

2 So you've dealt with the changes to the circle and square. What other shapes are left? Notice that the four triangles are the same size and in the same position in both diagrams. But they look different. How? They have been turned to point inwards in the second diagram.

3 You've now found the rules:
- Rule 1: The small central shape and large outer shape change places.
- Rule 2: The small triangles are rotated by 180°.

Given these rules, which of the five answer options completes the pair after the colon?

The easiest way is to eliminate answer options that can't be right. We can eliminate **e** as the small centre shape should be a hexagon. We can also get rid of **b** as the large outer shape should be a diamond. In **d** the large shape and triangles have been rotated by 45°, so **d** is not the answer. That leaves **a** and **c**, which are very similar and seem to follow most of the rules for making a pair. But look closely at the small triangles. Only **c** follows the final rule that the triangles are rotated to face the opposite direction.

Answer c

It helps me sometimes if I draw the shape that I'm looking for and then see which answer looks the closest.

Lalit

YOUR TURN

On the left of each of the rows below are two shapes with an arrow between them. Decide how the second is related to the first. After these there is a third shape, then an arrow and then five more shapes. Decide which of the five shapes goes with the third one to make a pair like the two on the left. Circle its letter.

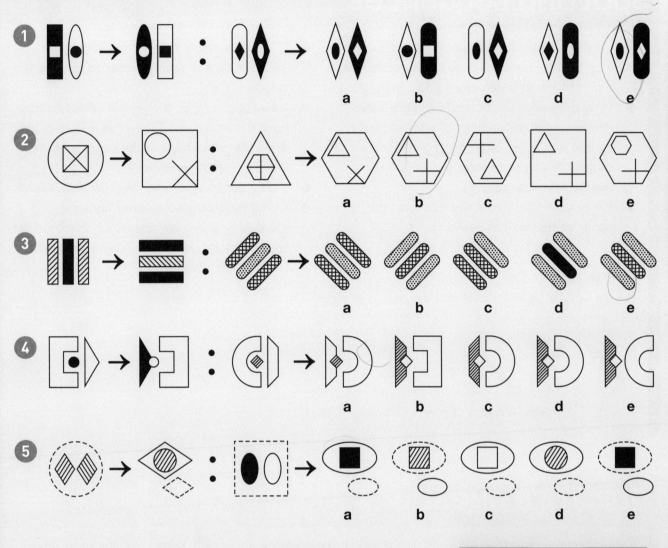

Answers | Progress Chart

55

non-verbal fun

Spotting sequences

This activity gets you thinking about series and rules by having to make up your own questions. Each person needs a pen and some paper.

- First, think of a solution rule to your series (for example, the number of sides increases by one and it has alternating black and white shapes). If you need ideas for rules, look at the Key Words (page 44).
- Write down your rule and fold over the paper so no one can see it.

- Under this, draw the first two shapes in your series. Ask your partner to guess the solution rule.
- If they get it right, they get 5 points and they have the next turn. If they get it wrong, you draw the next shape in the series and then ask them to guess again.
- If they get it right now, they get 4 points.
- Carry on until your partner finds the solution or you have drawn six shapes in the series. The quicker they find the solution, the more points they get.

How to play

Solution rule: Arrow rotates 90 degrees anti-clockwise

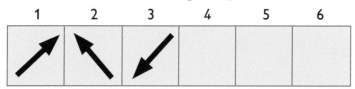

| 1 | 2 | 3 | 4 | 5 | 6 |

5 points 4 points 3 points 2 points 1 point

Quickfire questions

These quickfire questions will start you thinking about rotation and how things are like each other. This will build up the skills you need for these 11+ questions. Challenge your friends!

1. If you rolled the top 10p coin around the outside of the lower one, at what point would it be upside down? At what point would it be the right way up again? Try it.

2. Which row does K belong in? Why?

   A E F H I
   B C D G J

3. If a 1p coin changes to a 2p coin, what does a 5p coin change to? A £1 coin, a 50p coin, a 10p coin, a £2 coin or a 20p coin?

4. Here a large painted cube has been cut into 27 small cubes. On how many sides are the cubes A, B, C and D painted?

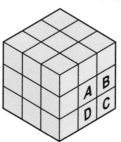

Answers ▶

3 CRACKING CODES

The two question types in this section involve matching code letters to features of diagrams. You have to work out which code letters belong to which part of the diagram from the clues you are given.

You will need to have an eye for detail, so that you can spot the small differences between the diagrams and you will need to work through the question systematically. Because you use the same skills for both question types, you are building up your skills all the time!

QUESTION TYPES

CRACK THE VERTICAL CODE

CRACK THE HORIZONTAL CODE

What will help me?

- Good understanding of rotation and position of shapes
- Noticing similarities in size
- Spotting similarities in shading
- Ability to compare similar-looking items and good observation skills to 'spot the difference'
- Making links between features of diagrams and symbols that represent them

3 STEPS TO SUCCESS

This 3-step method will help you solve all 11+ **CRACKING CODES** questions. It might seem a lot to do but, if you practise, you will soon be able to work through it quickly!

STEP 1   Look at one set of code letters. Find two or more diagrams that have the same letter. Work out which feature that letter must relate to in those diagrams. You are looking for a feature that only appears in the diagrams that have that letter (plus the feature will be different in diagrams that have different code letters).

STEP 2   Find the same feature in the test diagram, which will therefore have the same code letter. You have now found the first code letter of the answer. Write it down so you don't have to remember it. (The test diagram is the diagram that has no code letters, so you are trying to work out the code for it.)

STEP 3   Repeat Steps 1 and 2 for each set of code letters. By identifying which letters relate to which features, you will be able to find the answer code.

A Angles of rotation
N Number of sides, shapes and lines
S Size of shapes
W Where small shapes or lines are positioned
E Explore combinations of features and rules
R Reflection
S Shading

Remember the features to look for!

KEY WORDS

Diagram: describes a whole drawing. The words 'shape' and 'test shape' are used in the 11+ test, but we think that 'diagram' and 'test diagram' are easier to understand while learning how to do the questions. In CRACK THE HORIZONTAL CODE questions, a 'box' surrounds the diagram.

Shape: an individual shape, such as a square, hexagon, triangle or circle. A diagram can be made up of a single shape or a number of shapes.

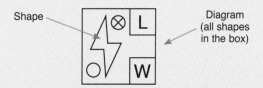

Shape ← | Diagram (all shapes in the box)

Rules and features: these are what make the difference, similarity, change or progression between diagrams. For example, a large circle may contain one small shape in the first diagram and then two in the next. So the rule 'one small shape inside the circle' would be linked to a particular code letter while 'two small shapes' would be represented by a different code letter.

Counting: often you will need to count the number of sides of a shape or the number of objects inside a bigger shape.

Overlap: where shapes are on top of each other. They can either be in front of or behind the other.

Positioning of shapes: where shapes are placed. For example, they can be above, below or to the sides and at angles to each other.

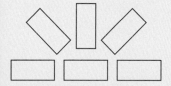

Reflection: where you can see a shape is the mirror image of another. Here the shape is reflected horizontally.

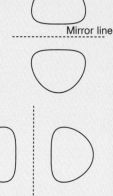

Mirror line

And here the shape is reflected vertically.

Mirror line

Rotation: where shapes are turned round. The angle of rotation tells you how the shapes have been rotated, for example by 45° each time here.

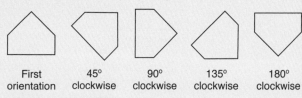

| First orientation | 45° clockwise | 90° clockwise | 135° clockwise | 180° clockwise |

Shading: how shapes are filled. Here you can see the shapes are filled with a solid shade, lines and then dots. Other shading may also be used, such as crosses or stars.

Symmetry: a line of symmetry through a shape is the line on which you could fold the shape perfectly in half. If it is a regular shape, then the number of lines of symmetry equals the number of sides. Some shapes have no lines of symmetry.

4 lines of symmetry | An infinite number of lines of symmetry | 1 line of symmetry | No lines of symmetry | 5 lines of symmetry

CRACK THE VERTICAL CODE

In these questions, you have to match codes to features of diagrams. First, you need to find features that are the same in different diagrams. Then you must work out which letter represents which feature. You will then be able to work out the code for another diagram.

It's a bit like doing detective work to find a secret code. So you will have to work carefully, but also quickly to make sure that you have time to answer as many questions as possible in the 11+ test.

In Non-Verbal Reasoning questions, code letters represent parts of the diagrams. But we use different sorts of codes a lot in our everyday life. They often appear as symbols.

Think about the weather. What do you think these symbols mean?

Symbols like this are often used in weather forecasts. We can usually 'crack the weather code' easily, as we know what these symbols mean. Try watching a weather forecast on TV without the sound on and see how well you understand it by just looking at the symbols.

11+ STYLE QUESTION

To answer these questions you have to work out a code. On the left are some shapes and the codes that go with them. You must decide how the code letters go with the shapes. Then find the correct code for the **test shape** from the set of five codes on the right.

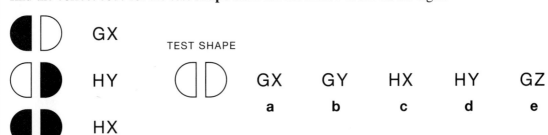

HOW TO DO IT

Follow the **3 steps to success** (from page 57) to work out the answer.

1. Look at one **column** of code letters, for example GHH. Remember that each letter stands for a particular feature in the diagram. The letters in the first column therefore represent one particular feature of the diagram, and the letters in the second column stand for another feature.

So, what do G and H stand for in the diagrams? Start by looking for things that are the same. The middle and bottom diagrams both have an H as the first letter of their code. Can you see anything the same in these two diagrams? The second semi-circle is shaded in each of these diagrams but, in the top diagram which has the code letter G, the second semi-circle is unshaded. We can now match H to shading and G to no shading in the second semi-circle.

2 Look at the test diagram and decide which code letter you need. It's G, no shading in the second semi-circle.

3 Now repeat Steps 1 and 2 for the code letters X and Y, which both also represent a unique feature. The top and bottom diagrams here both have an X in their code. What do these two diagrams have in common? The first semi-circle is shaded in both diagrams. So we can say that X means the first semi-circle is shaded and Y means the first semi-circle is not shaded.

In the test diagram neither of the semi-circles is shaded. Therefore the answer code must be G and Y, so option **b** is the correct answer.

Answer b

VARIATIONS

This question type may have some variations. They are likely to be similar to the examples shown below. Look at how the correct answer is worked out in these examples and you will be able to follow this approach if you come across variations like these.

No repeated letters

Sometimes you will find a set of codes where the letters are not repeated. For example, here S is repeated in the first column, but the letters LMNO are not repeated in the second column.

 RL

 SM

 TN

 SO

	RN	TM	SL	RM	TO
	a	b	c	d	e

Use the **3 steps to success** approach for working out what the first code letter will be (that is the first column RSTS in this case, as it's a vertical code question).

You can see that S means the second of the three triangles is shaded, while R means the central triangle is shaded and T means the outer triangle is shaded. The test diagram has the central triangle shaded, so R must be the first code letter in the answer.

The difference with the second set of vertical code letters is that none are repeated. So what can they represent? The only other feature that makes the diagrams different from each other is the direction in which they are facing. As they all appear in a different rotation, we can match the rotation of the test diagram to the second diagram and say that M must be the correct code letter. Answer option **d** (RM) is therefore the correct answer.

Other variations

- There are two types of vertical code question – one where you have to work out the codes using three example diagrams and another where four diagrams are given as examples.
- There may be two or three code letters to find.

This example shows you how to use the **3 steps to success** with a question that has four diagrams and three code letters.

JRX
KSY
JSZ
LTX

	KTX	JTZ	LSX	LRY	KTZ
	a	**b**	**c**	**d**	**e**

1 Look at one column of code letters, for example JKJL. You can see that the letter J appears next to two of the diagrams. Which feature does that letter relate to in these two diagrams? To find out, you have to look for something that is the same in both diagrams and is in the same position. Only the large square appears in both. If J stands for a large square, K must be the large circle and L the large hexagon.

2 In the test diagram the first large shape is a circle and therefore the first of the code letters must be K. Write down K. If you look at the answer options, we can eliminate **b**, **c** and **d** already because they don't include K. That leaves **a** and **e**.

3 Repeat Steps 1 and 2 for each column of code letters. Can you work out the correct answer option?

- S is repeated in the second column of code letters RSST. So we need to find the feature that S represents. The two diagrams with the S code letter have the large triangle in common. In the test diagram there is an oval, which is also in the bottom diagram. T must represent the oval. Write down T after the K you've already found. Both answer options that you have left, **a** and **e**, have a T as the second code letter.
- The final column of letters is XYZX. This means that the top and bottom diagrams must have something in common – the position of the small

It helps if I write down each letter as I work it out, especially if there are three different letters to remember.

Ali

black dot. In the test diagram the black dot appears inside the first large shape, as it does in the third diagram down on the left. Therefore, the code letter for the black dot must be Z. Write Z after the K and T.

Put all the code letters together to get KTZ – answer option **e**.

Answer e

YOUR TURN

To answer these questions you have to work out a code. On the left are some shapes and the codes that go with them. You must decide how the code letters go with the shapes. Then find the correct code for the **test shape** from the set of five codes on the right. Circle its letter.

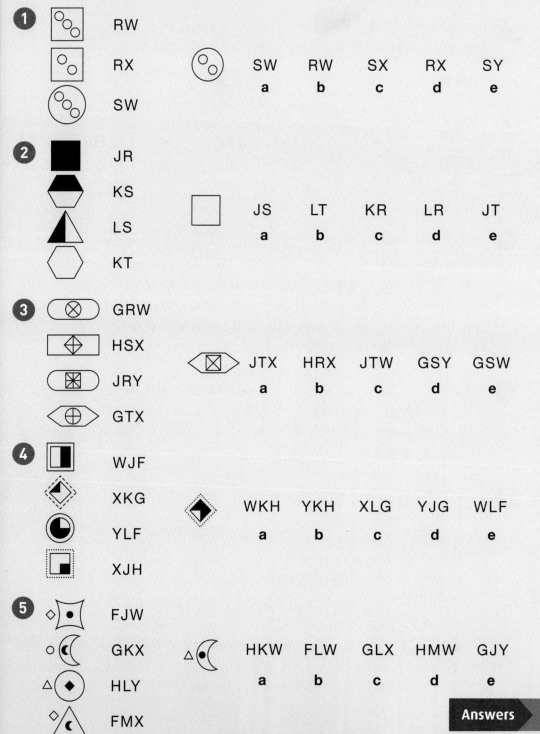

1

RW

RX

SW

SW   RW   SX   RX   SY
a   b   c   d   e

2

JR

KS

LS

KT

JS   LT   KR   LR   JT
a   b   c   d   e

3

GRW

HSX

JRY

GTX

JTX   HRX   JTW   GSY   GSW
a   b   c   d   e

4

WJF

XKG

YLF

XJH

WKH   YKH   XLG   YJG   WLF
a   b   c   d   e

5

FJW

GKX

HLY

FMX

HKW   FLW   GLX   HMW   GJY
a   b   c   d   e

Answers   **Progress Chart**

CRACK THE HORIZONTAL CODE

These questions are similar to vertical codes, but are shown horizontally. You are given three or four diagrams, with two code letters next to them. The code letters are *not* part of the diagram.

Again, you will need good observation skills and will need to work through each question carefully, step by step.

In these questions, the codes are letters, but remember that there are different sorts of codes all around us. For example, computers use symbols a lot. Look at the instruction below:

then

If you are familiar with computers, you may recognise 'save' and 'print' without even thinking about it, as you already know the code.

Look out for codes in the world around you. When you find a new code that you aren't familiar with, find out what it means.

11+ STYLE QUESTION

To answer these questions you have to work out a code. In the boxes on the left are shapes and the code letters that go with them. The top letters mean something different from the bottom ones. You must decide how the letters go with the shapes. Then find the correct code for the **test shape** from the set of five codes on the right.

TEST SHAPE

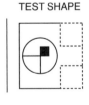

a   b   c   d   e

HOW TO DO IT

![steps icon] Follow the **3 steps to success** to work out the answer.

1 The code letters RST at the top of each box represent certain features of each diagram, as do the letters LMN at the bottom.

All the diagrams have a circle, a shaded square and two lines in the form of a quarter circle. The circle is the same in each box, but the square and quarter circle move around.

To work out the missing code letters in the test diagram, we need to find something that is the same in two of the diagrams. Two diagrams share the code letter R. What can you see that is the same in these two diagrams? The position of the quarter circle is the only feature that both diagrams have in common.

2 So the top code letter stands for the position of the quarter circle. The quarter circle of the test diagram is in the same place as the second diagram in the row, so the top letter in the answer is S. Only answer options **b** and **d** match this.

3 Looking at the bottom codes, the first and fourth diagrams share the code letter L. What do these diagrams have in common? It's the position of the shaded square inside the circle. The position of the square in the test diagram matches that of the third diagram in the row, so the bottom code letter for the test diagram must be N. The code for the test diagram therefore is SN, answer option **d**.

Answer d

A MORE DIFFICULT QUESTION

![steps icon] Use the **3 steps to success** to solve a more difficult question.

a   b   c   d   e

1 Look at the code letters at the top of the boxes. Find a letter that appears next to two or more diagrams. The first and third diagrams both have a letter L. The only feature that is the same in these diagrams and different from the other two diagrams is that the large lightning shape has a solid outline. So L must mean a solid outline, M a dashed outline and N a dotted outline.

2 In the test diagram the large lightning shape has a dashed line, so the top code letter must be M.

3 As we have worked out the large shape, that just leaves the circles at the top and bottom of the boxes to look at. Each of the circles at the bottom is the same, so they can't have anything to do with the bottom code letter. All the bottom code letters are different from each other and so are the circles at the top of each diagram. The circle at the top of the test diagram matches that of the first diagram. The missing bottom code letter must therefore be W. This gives us MW as our missing code and so answer option **b** is the correct answer.

Answer b

VARIATIONS

These questions can have variations. As we have just seen, not *all* parts of the diagrams are *always* relevant. Sometimes details are there just to distract you. Watch out for these! Have a look at how the correct answer is worked out in this example and you will be able to follow this approach if you come across variations like it.

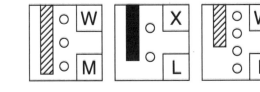
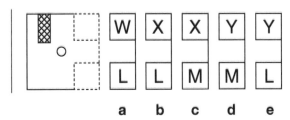

a   b   c   d   e

1 Start by trying the **3 steps to success** approach. First, work out whether the top code letter for the test diagram will be W, X or Y.

2 W is the top code letter for the first and third diagrams. The shading of the rectangle is the same in both of these diagrams. If the top code letter stands for the shading of the rectangle, then the test diagram must have Y as its top code letter, as it matches the fourth diagram. This means that you can eliminate answer options **a**, **b** and **c**, as they don't have a Y as the top code letter.

3 There are only two lower code letters, M and L. These could relate to the size of the rectangle or to the circles. There doesn't seem to be a consistent relationship between the letters and the size of the rectangle, so let's look at the circles. In the diagrams with code letter M, there are three and five circles. In the diagrams with code letter L, there are two and four circles. It would seem, therefore, that M stands for an odd number of circles and L an even number. As the test diagram has only one circle, its bottom code letter is M.

The answer code for the test diagram is therefore YM, answer option **d**.

Answer d

To answer these questions you have to work out a code. In the boxes on the left are shapes and the code letters that go with them. The top letters mean something different from the bottom ones. You must decide how the letters go with the shapes. Then find the correct code for the **test shape** from the set of five codes on the right. Circle its letter.

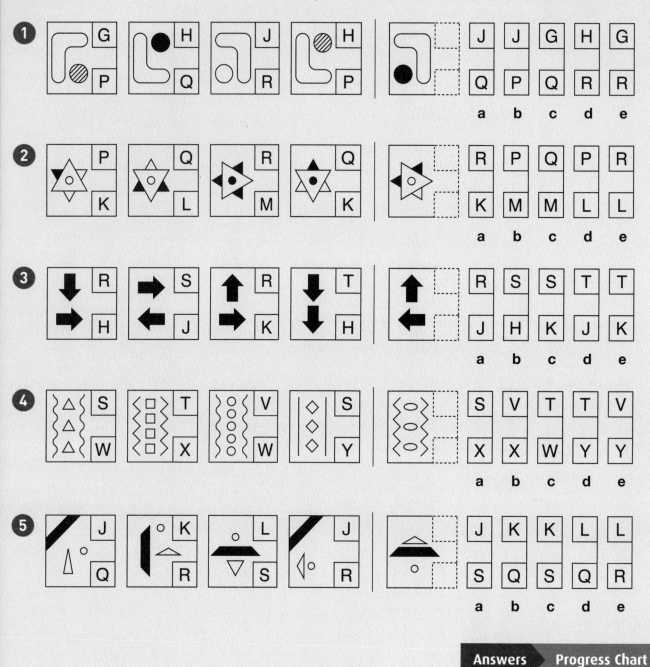

I always start by looking for shapes that have the same letter. That makes it easier for me to find the code.

Emily

non-verbal fun

Shape race

This is a timed challenge to see how quickly you can draw shapes following two different rules. It shows you how one rule can lead to many different shapes and how rules can be combined. Play it on your own, or challenge a family member or friend.

● Think of two rules that you will use to draw shapes. (If you're playing with a partner, think of a rule each.) The rules must describe common features of the shapes (for example, shapes have five sides, shapes have one quarter shaded, shapes have a curve, etc).

● Then draw two overlapping circles on a piece of A4 paper and write one rule above each circle, as shown below. If you're playing with a partner, each of you must draw the two overlapping circles, plus rules, on your own piece of paper.

● Each person has 2 minutes to draw in as many shapes that follow the rules as they can.

● Your shapes must follow Rule 1, Rule 2 or both Rules 1 and 2:
   – If a shape follows Rule 1, draw it in the left-hand circle.
   – If it follows Rule 2, draw it in the right-hand circle.
   – If it follows Rules 1 *and* 2, draw it in the middle.

● After 2 minutes, swap your paper with your partner for scoring. If you are playing on your own, ask your parent or carer to check your drawings.
   – Each shape that correctly follows Rule 1 or Rule 2 scores 1 point.
   – Each shape that correctly follows both Rules 1 and 2 (shapes in the middle) scores 2 points.
   – If any shapes are wrong and don't follow the rules correctly, take off 1 point.

● The winner is the person with the most points.

How to play

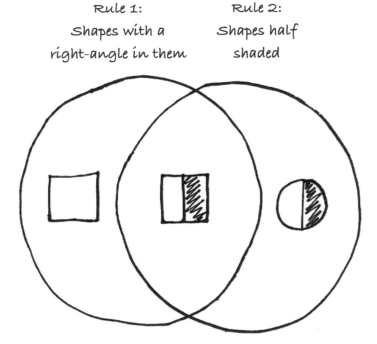

FIND THE ODD ONE OUT

1 

     a   **b**   **c**   **d**   **e**

d: The arrow points towards the circle in each diagram except **d**.

2

     a   **b**   **c**   **d**   **e**

b: The diagram contains only one small circle.

3      

     a   **b**   **c**   **d**   **e**

c: Each large shape contains three smaller shapes which may be shaded or unshaded or have a dashed outline. However, all except **c** have a square, a circle and a triangle. **c** has a circle, a triangle and an arch shape, but not a square.

4   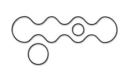

     a   **b**   **c**   **d**   **e**

a: All the diagrams have two circles plus another curved shape, but **a** has three circles.

5

     a   **b**   **c**   **d**   **e**

c: If you were only able to move the two shapes in each diagram in either a vertical or horizontal direction, you could make a perfect square from the cut-outs in the two shapes. In **c** you would have to twist, or rotate, one of the shapes by 180° in order to achieve this.

FIND THE DIAGRAM LIKE THE FIRST TWO

1

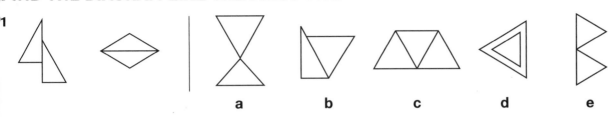

e: This diagram also has two triangles that are the same size.

2

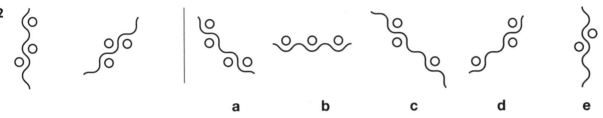

d: Each of the two curved lines are identical in length and have one circle on one side and two circles on the other side.

3

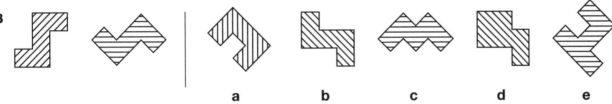

b: The two diagrams to the left of the line are identical to each other, as is **b**. Rotation is the only difference.

4

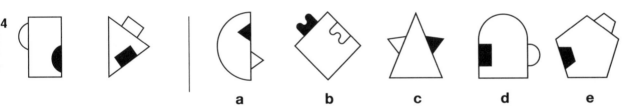

e: The two diagrams on the left each have a large shape with two smaller identical shapes attached to its outline. One small shape is inside the large shape and is shaded, while the other is outside the shape and is unshaded. The small shapes are on different sides of the large shape, so **a** cannot be the correct answer. Only **e** follows all the rules.

5

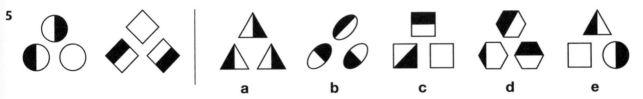

c: Both diagrams on the left of the line have three identical shapes, with two being half shaded. Only **c** follows these rules.

FIND THE DIAGRAM LIKE THE FIRST THREE

1

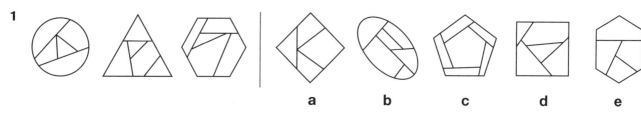

                                     a   **b**   **c**   **d**   **e**

d: Only **d** also has four lines crossing it, dividing it into five pieces.

2

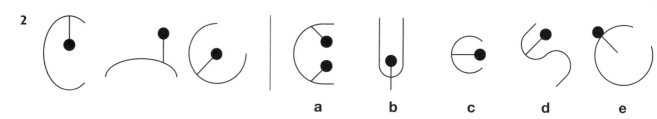

                                     a   **b**   **c**   **d**   **e**

c: The end point of one circle on a stick is connected to the inside or outside edge of a single curved shape.

3

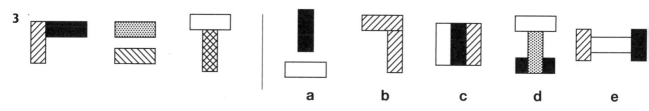

                                     a   **b**   **c**   **d**   **e**

a: Only **a** also has two rectangles, each with different shading.

4

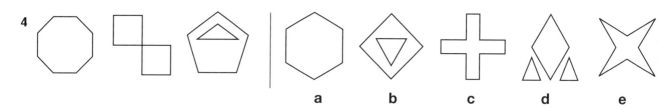

                                     a   **b**   **c**   **d**   **e**

e: Only **e** also follows the rule that the number of sides in each diagram add up to eight.

5

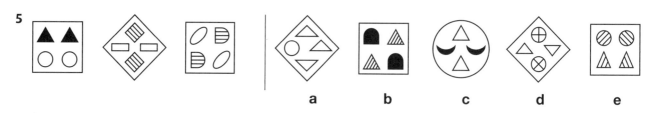

                                     a   **b**   **c**   **d**   **e**

b: Only **b** has two pairs of identical small shapes with the same shading inside a square like the first three diagrams.

NON-VERBAL FUN (Finding Similarities and Differences)

Quickfire questions

1. N is the only letter that doesn't have a vertical line of symmetry.
2. The most obvious difference is that the 50p has seven sides while all the others are perfect circles.
3. One possible answer is that the 2p coin is a different colour from the four silver-coloured coins. If you look for an underlying rule, all the coins represent an even number of pence except for the 5p, which represents an odd number.
4. The 10p is the one that belongs with the first three as it is the same colour.

COMPLETE THE SERIES

1

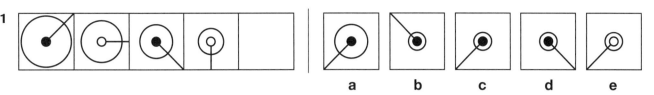

c: The large circle gets smaller from box to box. The small central circle alternates between shaded and unshaded. The line coming from the centre of the box rotates 45° clockwise each time.

2

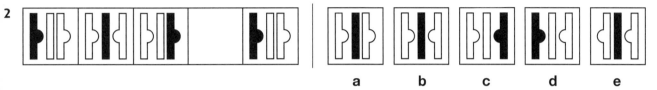

b: The first two of the three shapes in each box keep their position, but the third shape is reflected vertically. Shading of the shapes moves from the first shape to the second to the third and then back to the second and first, and so on.

3

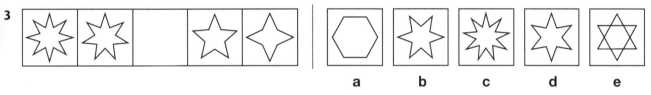

d: The number of points on the stars decreases by one each time. There is always a point facing directly upwards.

4

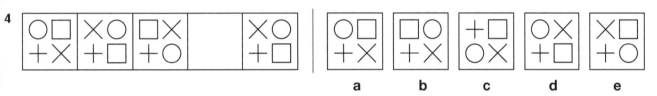

a: The plus symbol stays in the same place in each box. The three remaining shapes move clockwise one position at a time.

5

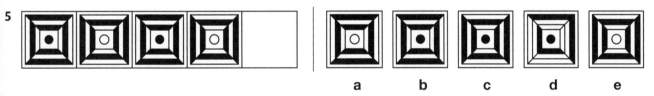

b: This may look a little complicated at first, but the answer is quite simple. There is a repeating pattern – box 1 is the same as boxes 3 and 5, while box 2 is the same as box 4.

COMPLETE THE GRID

1

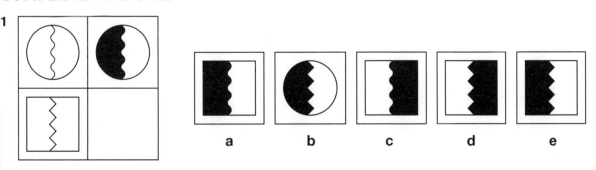

e: The diagram from the left-hand box is repeated in the right-hand box across the row, but with the left side of the diagram shaded.

2

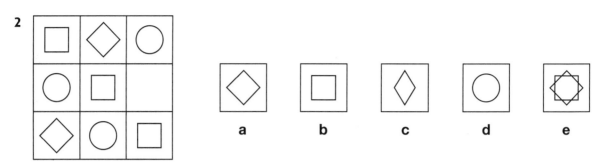

a: There should be three of each shape, one in each row and column as this is a Latin square.

3

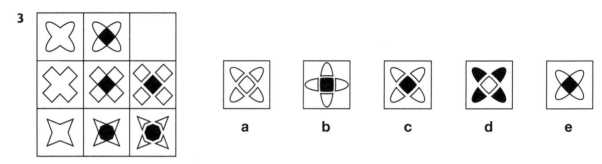

c: The diagrams change across the rows. First the shape is open, next the centre of the diagram is filled in, and then the whole diagram separates into five shapes.

4

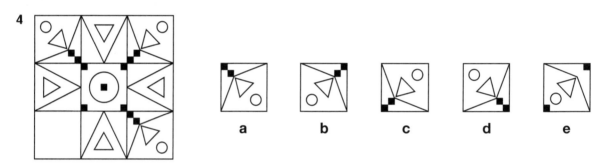

b: The pattern created over the whole grid is symmetrical in four directions. Only **b** fits this pattern.

5

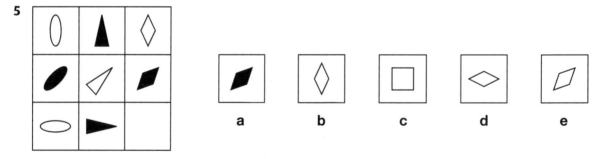

d: The shapes change orientation as you go down the columns. Each shape rotates 45° clockwise and changes shading from box to box.

COMPLETE THE PAIR

1

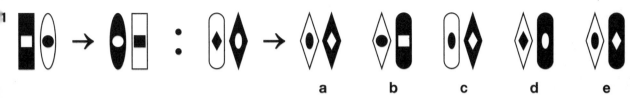

           a   **b**   **c**   **d**   **e**

e: The whole diagram is reflected vertically (that is, it flips across from left to right). Both the large and small shapes swap shading.

2

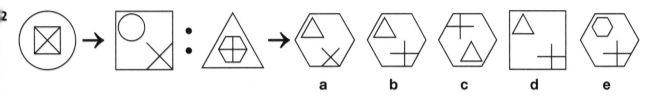

           a   **b**   **c**   **d**   **e**

b: The large outer shape gets smaller and moves into the top left corner of the new large outer shape. The new large outer shape is the small central shape from the first diagram. The pattern inside the first smaller shape goes to the bottom right in the second diagram.

3

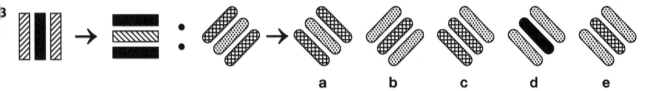

           a   **b**   **c**   **d**   **e**

e: The whole diagram rotates 90° clockwise. The middle and outer shapes swap shading.

4

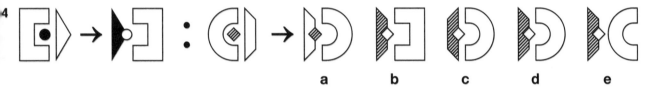

           a   **b**   **c**   **d**   **e**

d: The large shape at the left of the first diagram is reflected vertically (that is, it flips to the right) in the second diagram. The other two shapes swap shading. The small central shape moves to the centre at the right side of the right-hand shape.

5

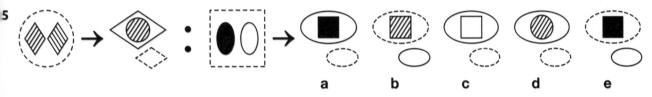

           a   **b**   **c**   **d**   **e**

a: The two shapes inside the large outer shape rotate by 90°. One of these shapes gets bigger and one gets smaller. The large outer shape gets smaller and sits inside the new larger shape, taking its shading from the original left-hand inner shape. The line style of the original large outer shape is applied to the remaining small shape.

NON-VERBAL FUN (Completing Diagrams)

Quickfire questions

1 A quarter of the way round; half way round

2 K belongs in the top row because it is made from straight lines only, like all the letters in the top row. The letters in the bottom row all have curves in them.

3 10p – the number doubles

4 A 1 side, B 2 sides, C 3 sides, D 2 sides

CRACK THE VERTICAL CODE

1

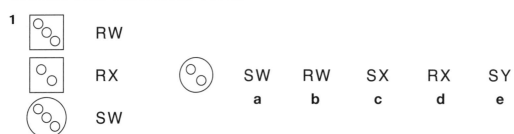

RW

RX

SW

SW   RW   SX   RX   SY
a   b   c   d   e

c: R and S represent the large outer shape. W and X represent the number of small circles inside the large shape.

2

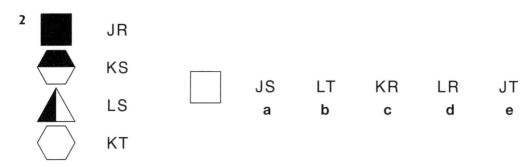

JR

KS

LS

KT

JS   LT   KR   LR   JT
a   b   c   d   e

e: J, K and L represent the type of shape: square, hexagon and triangle. R, S and T represent whether the shape is fully shaded, half-shaded or not shaded.

3

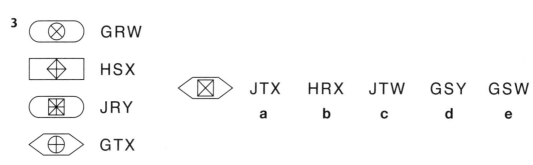

GRW

HSX

JRY

GTX

JTX   HRX   JTW   GSY   GSW
a   b   c   d   e

c: G, H and J represent the small circle, diamond and square inside the larger shapes. R, S and T represent the large shape. W, X and Y represent the way the small shape is filled in.

4

WJF

XKG

YLF

XJH

WKH   YKH   XLG   YJG   WLF
a   b   c   d   e

b: W, X and Y represent how much of the inner shape is shaded (half, quarter or three-quarters). J, K and L represent the inner shape. F, G and H represent the line style of the outer shape.

5

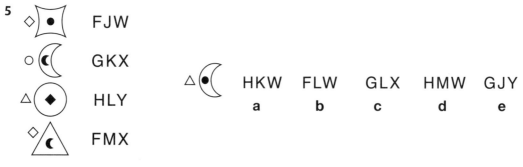

FJW

GKX

HLY

FMX

HKW   FLW   GLX   HMW   GJY
a   b   c   d   e

a: F, G and H represent the small shape on the left of each diagram. J, K, L and M represent the large shape. W, X and Y represent the small shaded shape inside the large shape.

CRACK THE HORIZONTAL CODE

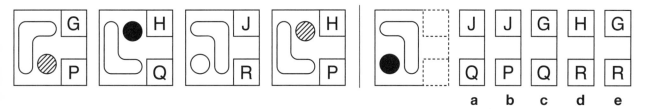

	a	b	c	d	e
top	J	J	G	H	G
bottom	Q	P	Q	R	R

a: G, H and J relate to the position, or orientation, of the large curved shape. P, Q and R relate to the shading of the circle.

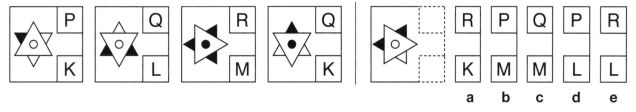

	a	b	c	d	e
top	R	P	Q	P	R
bottom	K	M	M	L	L

e: P, Q and R relate to the position, or orientation, of the triangles in the boxes. K, L and M relate to the number of small triangles shaded. The central circles are irrelevant and are there to distract you as no codes match the circles.

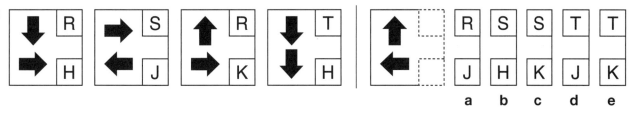

	a	b	c	d	e
top	R	S	S	T	T
bottom	J	H	K	J	K

c: R, S and T relate to the direction in which the bottom arrow is facing. H, J and K relate to the direction in which the top arrow is facing.

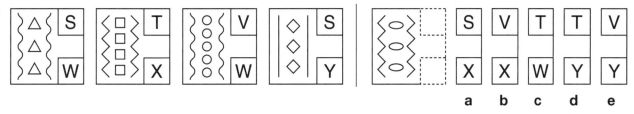

	a	b	c	d	e
top	S	V	T	T	V
bottom	X	X	W	Y	Y

a: S, T and V relate to the number of small shapes running down the centre between the two lines. W, X and Y relate to the style of lines.

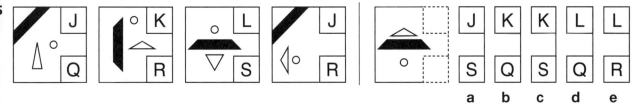

	a	b	c	d	e
top	J	K	K	L	L
bottom	S	Q	S	Q	R

e: J, K and L relate to the position of the thick black shape in the boxes. Q, R and S relate to the style of triangle. The circle is irrelevant and is only there to distract you.

PROGRESS CHART

TARGET	TARGET	TARGET	TARGET	TARGET	TARGET	TARGET	TARGET
Brilliant effort. Always check answers.			Great, you are getting there. Watch your favourite TV programme tonight.		Well done, you've reached the target!	Brilliant effort. Listen to your music for half an hour.	
Apply a good technique to each question.		Apply a good technique to each question.		Apply a good technique to each question			Apply a good technique to each question.
	Make sure the answers make sense.		Make sure the answers make sense.			Make sure the answers make sense.	
		You've made a good start. Keep working at it.			You've made a good start. Keep working at it.		You've made a good start. Keep working at it.
Double-check the 'how to do it' section.				Double-check the 'how to do it' section.			
Find the Odd One Out	**Find the Diagram Like the First Two**	**Find the Diagram Like the First Three**	**Complete the Series**	**Complete the Grid**	**Complete the Pair**	**Crack The Vertical Code**	**Crack the Horizontal Code**

1 FINDING SIMILARITIES AND DIFFERENCES	**2 COMPLETING DIAGRAMS**	**3 CRACKING CODES**

How to use your Progress Chart

- Every time you complete the 'Your Turn' questions, check the answers at the back of this book.
- Then colour this Progress Chart to show how many questions you got correct for that question type. If you want, you could use stickers instead.
- This will show you how well you are doing and will also point out the question types that you need to practise again.
- If you haven't coloured in the whole bar for a question type, then go back to the 'Your Turn' section. Finish off any questions that you missed out or try some again if you got them wrong.
- Start at the bottom and when you reach the final question, colour in the target, too. Well done! You've got there.